Dating!

10 HELPFUL TIPS
for a Successful Relationship

Laura Buddenberg, MS
Alesia K. Montgomery

BOYS TOWN.
Press

Boys Town, Nebraska

Dating! 10 Helpful Tips for a Successful Relationship
Published by Boys Town Press
14100 Crawford St., Boys Town, NE 68010
Copyright © 2012, Father Flanagan's Boys' Home
ISBN 978-1-934490-52-5

Boys Town Press is the publishing division of
Boys Town, a national organization serving
children and families.

Publisher's Cataloging-in-Publication Data

Buddenberg, Laura J.
  Dating! : 10 helpful tips for a successful relationship / written by Laura
J. Buddenberg and Alesia K. Montgomery. – Boys Town, NE : Boys
Town Press, c2013.

  p. ; cm.

  ISBN: 978-1-934490-52-5

  Audience: grades 7-12 (ages 13-18).
  Summary: Written in a clever "top 10 tips" format, the authors recount
actual teen dating stories, and explain the skills required to thrive in
relationships. A great resource to help teens and the caring adults in
their lives decipher the world of successful dating.--Publisher.

  1. Dating (Social customs) 2. Interpersonal relations in adolescence. 3.
Interpersonal attraction. 4. Teenage girls--Conduct of life. 5. Teenage
girls--Psychology. 6. Teenage boys--Conduct of life. 7. Teenage boys--
Psychology. 8. Parenting. 9. Parent and teenager. I. Montgomery, Alesia
K. II. Title. III. Title: 10 helpful tips for a successful relationship. IV.
Title: Ten helpful tips for a successful relationship.

HQ801 .B8746 2013
306.73/0835--dc23   1309

10 9 8 7 6 5 4 3 2 1

Boys Town National Hotline®
1-800-448-3000
A crisis, resource and referral number for kids and parents

YourLifeYourVoice.org
A website offering kids, teens, and young adults a
way to express feelings and seek help

TABLE OF CONTENTS

ACKNOWLEDGMENTS

We'd like to extend our deepest appreciation to the young people and families, in our personal and professional lives, who shared their relationship dreams, challenges, heartaches and successes with us. Their candor and stories form the backbone of this book.

We want to thank our department directors, Kathy Kirby and Erin Green, and department manager, Susan Lamke, for their professional guidance and support. We extend a special thank you also to our colleagues at the Boys Town National Hotline, our editor Brent Robinson, and our graphic artist, Anne Hughes. And last, but certainly not least, we express deep gratitude to Father Steven Boes and Boys Town leadership for their commitment to our mission of "Changing the way America cares for children, families and communities by providing and promoting an Integrated Continuum of Care® that instills Boys Town values to strengthen body, mind and spirit."

*** To Our Families ***

All my love and thanks to my husband, Roger, and our beautiful daughters, Cate and Claire. You teach me about love and relationships every day!
    – LAURA

I would like to thank my wonderful husband, Greg, and my lovely daughter, Jessica, for their patient support and encouragement throughout this project. I love you both!
    – ALESIA

What Makes a Good or a Bad Relationship?

What's your status? Single? In a Relationship? It's Complicated? How do you change your status? Is it possible to have relationships without getting hurt or hurting someone else? The truth is that dating relationships can make you happy or bring you down. But, here's the good news about dating: healthy, happy relationships aren't random.

There's even more good news.

You have the power to decide.

You can:

⭐ Discover if a relationship isn't good for you and walk away from it

⭐ Build a healthy relationship from the "ground" up

⭐ Take a good relationship and make it even better

It all comes down to skills, _knowledge_ and choices. You need to:

1 develop the skills to build fulfilling relationships that make you a better, happier person

2 know the facts and danger signs that signal relationship trouble

3 choose to date only those people who share your relationship values and demonstrate they "have the skills" for healthy relationships.

If you're dating now, have ever dated, have never dated, or hope to date (at some point in your life!) this book is for you. We'll give you 10 tips for successful dating relationships.

In each chapter, you'll read a couple's "relationship" story. Some of the relationships are positive, and some are not. All of the stories offer some wisdom on how to create or maintain a healthy relationship (or recognize when it's time to end an unhealthy one). Many situations may remind you of your own experiences in the dating world.

You also learn specific skills to help you along the way. Each chapter contains relationship facts (including how to navigate dating relationships in The Wired World) and highlights "danger signs" that tell you when to get out and move on before you really get hurt.

Hopefully, this book will help you think about your own experiences and relationships.

We want to begin with a story of a dating relationship that starts out good, but finishes very bad. See if you can relate to some of the things this young couple is experiencing. What would keep it a good relationship and what made it turn bad?

◈ ◈ ◈

Carrie started her sophomore year at a new school. It took several weeks for her to learn her way around and get to know people, but by October she had a nice group of friends.

Trevor, one of the guys in the group, was a junior. He played on the varsity football team and seemed to know and get along with everyone. Carrie thought he was cute, easy to talk to, and really funny. She always enjoyed herself when he was around.

By January they were spending time alone together, apart from the group. As soon as they started dating, she explained to him that she didn't believe in having sex in high school and asked him to respect her boundaries. He wholeheartedly agreed. She appreciated how open she could be with him, and was glad finally to be dating someone who didn't pressure her and who shared her values.

He told her he wanted to keep their relationship a secret, at least for a while. He said he didn't want other people "in their business" and gossiping about them. She said that was okay with her, but she really liked Trevor and found it hard not to talk about their relationship with her girlfriends.

In late February it was time for the winter formal dance. Trevor and Carrie decided that would be the perfect moment to make their relationship public. Their friends were happy for them, and so were Carrie's parents. Trevor spent lots of time around Carrie's family and they liked him very much. By the same token, Trevor's parents thought Carrie was a sweet girl and a good influence on Trevor.

Things between Carrie and Trevor were great – until April. Trevor picked Carrie up one Friday night and took her to a party. When they got there, she noticed several kids were drinking, and no parents were in sight. Trevor recognized how uncomfortable Carrie was, and asked her if she'd take a walk on the nearby golf course with him. She knew he'd been drinking, so she said no. In front of several of their friends, Trevor suddenly got angry, called Carrie a "slut" and pushed her so hard she fell and hit her head on the coffee table.

A girlfriend took Carrie home. She didn't want her parents to know she'd been at a party where underage kids were drinking, so when they asked her how she got the bruise on her forehead, she lied. Trevor called the next day, begging to see her. He apologized and told her he'd acted that way only because he'd been drinking, and it would never, ever happen again. She accepted his apology and they stayed together.

A few weeks later, Trevor started criticizing the way Carrie dressed. He told her that her clothes were too short and too tight, and he insisted she change before they went out together. Carrie thought he probably was right and she appreciated that he wanted her to look nice.

Not too long after that, Carrie and Trevor met friends at someone's house and they all enjoyed a movie night. Carrie was on the couch, with Trevor sitting right in front of her on the floor. She laughed out loud during one scene, and couldn't stop giggling. Trevor called her stupid, and then elbowed her hard in the gut. She felt humiliated and hurt and a friend ended up taking her home.

The next day, Trevor came over to see Carrie and acted like nothing had happened. When Carrie tried to tell him that he'd embarrassed her the night before, he shrugged and said he was "only kidding around" and Carrie was being too sensitive.

Carrie didn't know what to do. She realized she was starting to walk on eggshells around Trevor. She never was sure what his mood would be, or how he'd treat her. She tried talking to a girl he'd dated the year before, but that girl just said her advice would be to stay away from him.

Not knowing where to turn, she talked with her counselor at school, Mrs. Smith. For the first time, she admitted to being just a bit afraid of Trevor. Mrs. Smith convinced her to tell her older sister, Ruth, what was happening, and then to enlist Ruth to help her tell her parents. She also told Carrie to avoid being alone with Trevor.

Carrie took Mrs. Smith's advice. With her parents at her side, she called Trevor and broke up with him. After a few awkward weeks at school, Trevor moved on and Carrie realized she felt better than she had in months.

CHAPTER

1

ReLatioNSHip Status
WHat's yours?

Marcus and Shania first met in seventh grade. They had a couple of classes together and some mutual friends so they occasionally hung out as part of a larger group, but didn't really talk much at all. Over the next few years they ran into each other in class and at some school sporting events.

Their sophomore year in high school they both started working on the school newspaper. They talked about the stories they were working on and shared feedback on each other's work.

They saw each other every day and found they had lots in common. Marcus was the oldest of three boys in his family and Shania had a younger sister. They each really liked basketball, to play and to watch, and they were in chorus together, too. Shania told Marcus she thought he had a wonderful singing voice and encouraged him to try out for the all-state chorus.

By Christmas of that year, Marcus realized how much he looked forward to the time he spent with Shania. He thought she was

Say Whaaat?

"You have to walk carefully in the **beginning of love;** the running across fields into your lover's arms can only come later when you're sure they won't laugh if you trip."

— JONATHAN CARROLL

easy to talk to and very pretty. Shania thought Marcus was cute and funny. They had the same lunch period and started sitting together every day.

When they got back to school after winter break, Marcus asked Shania to a Friday night school basketball game. She explained to him that her family had a rule that any guy she went out with had to come to the door and meet her parents before she could leave the house with him. Marcus was nervous about this, but he showed up at her door, shook her Dad's hand, introduced himself and spent a little time talking with her parents before they headed out to the game. He assured them that he'd get her home by her 11:45 p.m. curfew.

They cheered on the team, enjoyed time with their friends, and talked all evening. After the game they went out for tacos with two other couples. They watched the time and Marcus made sure Shania was home when he promised her parents she would be.

After that night they started seeing a lot of each other, and all of their friends and others at school recognized them as a couple. They spent time alone, but often included other friends, too. They both were happy and liked being together.

Dating and relating. Sometimes fun, sometimes confusing. Relationships can help you learn about yourself and others and bring a lot of joy and comfort to your life. And, sometimes, relationships can be dangerous and bring a lot of pain to your life.

Before you change your status from "Single" to "In a Relationship", it's important to know yourself first, and to think about whether or not you're ready to "put yourself out there."

So let's say you've mastered some basic social skills, have talked with your parents and other adults you trust, and feel ready to tackle dating. You probably have lots of questions.

How do you know if you're in a good relationship? How do you know if you're in a relationship for the right reasons? Can you tell when someone really likes you or just is using you? How do you know if you're in over your head?

This book will help you answer some of these questions. We'll share tips and talk about the skills you need to get the relationships you want, as well as what you need to know to avoid being a "dating danger" to yourself and others. We'll look, too, at the benefits and pitfalls of technology when it comes to building relationships.

Some people think good relationships happen by accident – maybe you meet the right person and it all "clicks" and maybe you don't and things go wrong. The big key here is that, as the old saying goes, finding the right person (and relationship) starts with being the right person. In other words, to paraphrase Napoleon Dynamite, "You gotta have skills."

Take Marcus and Shania, for example. They're off to a great start. They have lots in common. They have mutual friends and they show respect for each other and for each other's families. So far, it looks like they know how to start a good relationship and keep it going. They're getting better and better at the skill of Maintaining Relationships.

There are lots of stages to "dating" relationships. A solid foundation in one stage sets you up for success in the next stage.

STAGE 1 Platonic Friendships

Before you start dating, the first stage is learning how to be and have friends. Many teens have discovered that they have more fun in school just being good friends together – hanging around and having fun in a group, without the pressure of dating. In such friendships, you can learn a lot not only about the others, but also about yourself, and ultimately about how to best communicate with, understand, and be friends with a future dating partner or spouse.

STAGE 2 Friendly Dating

It is only when you have mastered the skills needed for the first dating stage that you should move on to Stage 2. In order to participate in *Stage 2: Friendly Dating,* you must be very clear about your own physical, emotional,

Say Whaaat?

"Love is a fire. But whether it is going to warm your heart or burn down your house, you can never tell."
– JOAN CRAWFORD

sexual, and spiritual boundaries. And, you must be able to communicate these boundaries to those you will date.

Friendly dating will most likely involve spending time with and practicing friendship skills with someone to whom you are attracted. For friendly dating to remain friendly, each person must maintain healthy physical and sexual boundaries.

Talk to your parents or another trusted adult about how far is far enough – how physically and sexually close you should get to someone you are friendly dating. Maintaining clear boundaries regarding limited physical and sexual closeness can free you to really get to know one another and to practice the rules for good boundaries. Limiting physical and sexual closeness helps you to develop important skills like saying and accepting "no," exhibiting sexual self-control, and respecting others' boundaries.

Friendly dating can happen in a group or as a single date. But it always implies that you are getting to know and going out with various people. In other words, friendly dating is "dating around." It is not an exclusive relationship.

If you want to keep it friendly make sure to avoid:

★ **Couple behavior** – Exclusive dating, "hooking up," exchanging gifts like jewelry, clothing or stuffed animals, only walking with, only talking to, or always thinking about this one person, writing romantic or sexual notes, hanging all over each other

★ **Grooming tactics** – Jealousy and possessiveness, insecurity, intimidation, anger, accusation, bribery, flattery, status, or control

Keeping it friendly helps you to keep your options open and date around without hurting or using others. It keeps your reputation clean and helps you steer clear of giving mixed messages. It lets you meet, get to know, and perhaps even become friends with several people of the opposite gender while avoiding messy and painful breakups.

STAGE 3 Steady Friendly Dating

It is possible that while friendly dating you may meet one person that you would like to get to know even better. After a period of friendly dating of this person and others, the two of you decide to friendly date only one another. This is *Stage 3: Steady Friendly Dating*.

Teens who are ready for this dating stage are teens who demonstrate the following skills – they are able to set and communicate clear boundaries and limits, have self-control, are able to resist peer pressure, can handle their sexuality and frustration appropriately, can express feelings appropriately, and show self-respect and respect for others.

It is extremely important that teens involved in serious steady friendly dating do not limit themselves to spending time only with their boyfriend or girlfriend. Now more than ever before, these teens need to spend a good amount of time with other male and female friends, as well as with family, so that their boundaries remain firm and priorities clear.

STAGE 4 Serious Steady Dating

This type of dating relationship is not for high school teens. It is in this dating stage when you begin to ask yourself: Is this the spouse for me? Do I really love this person? Does he or she really love me? It is at this stage that the couple begins to examine the relationship in light of marriage.

> **re·la·tion·ship** *noun*
> source: dictionary.com
> 1. a connection, association, or involvement.
> 2. connection between persons by blood or marriage.
> 3. an emotional or other connection between people

STAGE 5 Engagement

At this time, the couple begins preparing to create and share a life together. Discussions about finances, in-laws, conflict resolution, child-rearing, etc., need to happen now. The focus should be on preparing for the future, not just for the wedding day.

STAGE 6 Marriage

For most people, marriage is the ultimate goal of dating. If all the previous stages have been followed, friendship skills have been mastered, each have maintained appropriate boundaries, and a real love for and commitment to the other person exists, then the couple will have an excellent chance of achieving a lasting, loving marriage.

 RELATIONSHIP SKILL **Maintaining Relationships**

1. **Frequently ask for feedback and be willing to accept it**

    Marcus and Shania talk all the time; they trade feedback on their newspaper stories, and are comfortable sharing thoughts and feelings.

2. Express concern and appropriate affection

Marcus and Shania show respect for themselves and each other by following their families' rules, like curfew and meeting the parents first.

3. Negotiate and compromise on activities

They don't always want to go to the same places, but can talk through their differences and come to a decision that's acceptable to both of them.

4. Share attention with others and avoid possessive and exclusionary behaviors

They spend lots of time with friends and family – balancing "alone" time with time with others.

ReLatioNSHip QUiZ

Please answer the following questions about the person you are in a relationship with (or someone you'd like to date). Your response can be agree, disagree, or not sure.

1. We are very supportive of each other's activities.

Agree   Disagree   Not Sure

2. We give each other plenty of social freedom with our friends.

Agree   Disagree   Not Sure

3. We are both great listeners when it comes to problem solving.

Agree   Disagree   Not Sure

4. Our friends approve of us being a couple.

Agree   Disagree   Not Sure

5. We both are involved in multiple activities and support each other.

   Agree   Disagree   Not Sure

6. What are some sure signs of a healthy relationship?

   a. respect

   b. true acceptance

   c. allowing individuality

   d. supportive of dreams

   e. encouraging personal growth

   f. all of the above

Now, go back and look at your answers. What "stage" do you think the relationship is in now? Do your answers reflect that, most of the time, you're comfortable sharing your thoughts and feelings, being supportive of each other, giving each other space, and including your family and friends in some of your activities together? If so, you are probably in a healthy relationship.

The Wired World

Remember, real relationships happen in real space; in other words, you need to spend time face-to-face to really get to know someone. You can text each other, or talk "online," but that should never replace talking or spending time together, including time with family and friends.

It's risky to start a relationship online because all you really know about someone you're talking to via text, social networking or chat is that the person has access to a "wired" device at that time. You can't see a face, hear a voice, watch the person around family or friends. It's easy for someone to "fake it" online, so make sure your relationships start face-to-face.

DANGER SIGNS

Confused About Our Relationship

My boyfriend and I broke up about a month or two ago. He said it was because we never hung out, or hardly talked. About three weeks ago he apologized a hundred times, and said I was "the beautifulest person in his life," and "he made the biggest mistake ever when he broke up with me."

Since I still love him; I went back out with him. We talked that whole week about loving and missing each other. Every other day the next week we sent messages when we could. Now he hasn't talked to me in almost a week. Every time I give him a hug, it's from the side... I'm confused? Help?

We hardly ever talk in person. It's always over Facebook. How can we get more comfortable talking in person?

A Relationship Or An Obsession?

"I think I'm obsessed with my love. We're 15, but really mature and we love each other. We can't be together until I'm 16 so I always feel the need to text him constantly and just always think about him and depend my happiness on him. Every little thing gets me jealous even if he just talks to a girl. Every little mistake he makes I point out. I do it because I feel like when he makes a mistake, it's because he doesn't love me anymore. It's hard to explain.

When I'm not talking to him I feel empty and I'm so afraid I will lose him to another girl. I'm just really obsessed with him and feel that my happiness depends on him. I guess I'm insecure about myself."

Whoa! These girls are in relationship trouble. The first one can't figure out what's really happening because she and her boyfriend aren't talking face-to-face, so she's missing most of the communication.

The second girl hasn't built a strong foundation of friendship skills, so her boyfriend is her "everything." Building your life around another person can lead to out-of-control jealousy and heartache for everyone involved. It looks like she needs a timeout to learn relationship skills so she can avoid trouble.

source: dictionary.com

sta·tus *noun*
1. the position of an individual in relation to another or others, especially in regard to social or professional standing.
2. state or condition of affairs

CHAPTER 2

TIP Kind Intentions

FroM SiNgLe to IN a ReLatioNSHip
KiNd (Not CrUeL) InteNtioNS

Cody and Katie, both seniors in high school, have been going out for a few months. They met at church youth group. He liked her smile and kindness; she was attracted to his blue eyes and sense of humor.

Katie went out with another guy during her sophomore year. He never wanted to spend time with friends or family – he always wanted to be alone with Katie and expected her to spend all of her free time with him. He encouraged her to lie to her parents so they could spend extra time together. When Katie tried to tell him she felt smothered in the relationship, he would get sullen, pout, and refuse to talk with her for days. Eventually, she broke up with him, and she told her friends it felt like a big relief to "get my life back!"

Katie doesn't want to make the same mistake with Cody. She told him upfront that her friends and family are important to her, and she wants Cody to know and like them – and vice-versa. She explained what happened in her earlier relationship, and answered Cody's questions honestly and completely.

Cody agrees that it's best to be open and honest. He and Katie make sure to have a balance between "alone time" and time with others who care about them. They have an "honesty is the best policy" agreement — they don't lie to each other or to their parents.

Katie has the right idea. Healthy relationships are based on trust – and you can't have trust without honesty.

Things go better with trust. For example, you're having an innocent conversation with a girl in your science class and your girlfriend sees you. Does she go a little bit crazy and accuse you of cheating on her? Or does she calmly join you and introduce herself because she knows this person is just a friend of yours? If you're with someone who gets emotional in every potential situation, or continuously accuses you of cheating, then there's a key ingredient missing in your relationship – trust.

Trust is built up over time as you prove you can rely and depend on each other. You should do what you say you'll do and be open and honest. You can't have a healthy relationship if you don't trust each other.

So, how do you know if someone is trustworthy? Here are some tips:

Trustworthy people:

1. **Tell the truth** – even when it's difficult.

2. **Keep appropriate confidences** – they don't gossip about you or others.

3. **Don't lie to parents, other adults, or their friends** – if your significant other lies to someone else, what's to keep him/her from lying to you? In other words, how many lies does someone have to tell before he/she is a liar?

4. **Keep their word** – they do what they say they're going to do when they say they're going to do it – they keep commitments.

5. **Never encourage you to do something that would hurt the people who love you most** – they don't stand between you and your family and other friends.

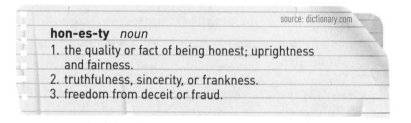

source: dictionary.com

hon-es-ty *noun*
1. the quality or fact of being honest; uprightness and fairness.
2. truthfulness, sincerity, or frankness.
3. freedom from deceit or fraud.

Say Whaaat?

"Only your **real friends** will tell you when your face is dirty."

– SICILIAN PROVERB

RELATIONSHIP SKILL — Communicating Honestly

1. **Look at the person**

   Because the conversation was important, Katie made sure she talked with Cody in person.

2. **Use a clear voice**

   Avoid stammering or hesitating. She was straightforward and calm when sharing her feelings.

3. **Respond to questions factually and completely**

   She said what she had to say and then asked Cody for his thoughts and questions.

4. **Do not leave out details or important facts**

   She was honest, and answered all questions completely.

5. **Truthfully take responsibility for your own behaviors**

   Katie didn't bash her former boyfriend – she shared her thoughts and feelings without putting him down or gossiping.

Relationship Facts

On an average, women say over 7,000 words per day. Men manage just over 2,000.

Studies show that happiness is contagious and that potential dates find it hard to walk away from happy people. One of the biggest turnoffs during a date is negativity.

Remember that having different opinions and ideas is ok. Avoiding conflict is not necessarily healthy. Resolving disagreements in a respectful way can be a sign of a healthy relationship.

The Wired World

It can be hard to know if someone's trustworthy and honest when you're communicating with them or getting to know them online. Remember, the only thing you know for sure about someone you're talking with online (or via texting!) is that they have access to an internet-capable device at that time.

When you're online, don't share lots of private thoughts and feelings. Also, take everything said online "with a grain of salt."

If what you have to say really is important, make the time to talk face-to-face. If that isn't possible (and it's so important it can't wait) then at least talk voice-to-voice.

Say Whaaat?

"Trust is the highest form of human motivation. It brings out the very best in people. But it takes time and patience."
– STEPHEN R. COVEY

Say Whaaat?

"Love cannot live where there is no trust."
— EDITH HAMILTON

source: dictionary.com

trust·wor·thi·ness *noun*
1. deserving of trust or confidence;
   dependable; reliable

When you can't communicate honestly, you can't establish trust. That can lead to anxiety for both of you. If you don't talk, you're operating on either too little information or, in the worst case, the wrong information.

The girl in the next story is a good example. She's operating on very little information and it's costing her.

My boyfriend and I have been dating for 10 months today, and I'm so attached. I seriously want to spend the rest of my life with him. It seems like I am smothering him. He always comments about not hanging out with his friends, and that we spend too much time together. I honestly agree, but I don't want to spend time without him.

I feel lost and depressed without him. If I give him space, will he take advantage of that and go out and do things I don't want him to be doing? I'm always wondering what he is doing. I have really bad trust issues and I don't know what to do.

This girl is miserable – and it sounds like her boyfriend isn't too happy, either. She doesn't give her boyfriend any time or space away from her, but she can't bring herself to express her fears and feelings. If she continues to keep everything inside, he'll get tired of being smothered and break up with her. On the other hand, if she calms down and shares what's bothering her they might have a chance at staying together. Either way, honest communication is the key to getting it resolved.

Say Whaaat?

"We all need to know what it means to be honest. Honesty is more than not lying. It is truth telling, truth speaking, truth living, and truth loving."

– JAMES E. FAUST

CHAPTER 3

Compliments

ReLatioNSHip CompLiMeNtS
Not CoN GaMeS (FLattery)

Tamika was a shy girl who sat in the back of her high school classroom hoping that no one would notice her. Trina, her older sister, attends the same school. She is the polar opposite of Tamika – outgoing, confident, and very popular.

Tamika loves her sister, but gets sad because Trina frequently receives invitations to parties and special events. Tamika never gets invited. Students usually make comparisons between the two sisters. Tamika would often hear her classmates say, "Trina is so pretty," or "Too bad Tamika doesn't look or act like her sister!"

The only time Tamika would hear compliments was when guys used flattery to see if they could "hook-up" with her. She would hear comments like, "Girl, you are the hottest thing around here, how 'bout we hook up later!" or "I want to get with you now." One older guy in her neighborhood recently told her that he loved how she "moved her hips" as she walked past him.

27

DATING!

Tamika ignored any compliments she received from guys because most of them were trying to flatter her for the wrong reasons. She recognized their con games from miles away!

The following week, David, a transfer student, walked through the student lounge and noticed Tamika tutoring freshmen algebra students after school. He marveled at her knowledge, wit, and friendly personality. She seemed to be in her "element." Unfortunately, her peers never realized how talented she was. David noticed her engaging smile, thoughtful responses, and concern for other students. Those qualities were very attractive to him! He told himself to "stop staring at this girl or she might think that you're weird."

As Tamika finished her tutoring session, she looked up and noticed a tall attractive young man staring at her. As she walked out of the building, David introduced himself and complimented her on how well she ran the tutoring session. He was impressed with how she motivated and engaged her students.

She thanked him for his kind words, then walked away saying to herself, "Oh my God! Here we go again, another slick dude trying to play me." David noticed her hesitance, so he backed off and gave her space. Several weeks went by before Tamika realized that David was an honest guy, who actually was sincere with his compliments and feelings towards her. She decided to initiate a conversation with him after school that day, and they have been exclusive friends ever since.

Say Whaaat?

"All you need is love.
But a little chocolate now and then doesn't hurt."
— CHARLES M. SCHULZ

Good for Tamika! She finally discovered that there are nice guys out there who are looking for a self-confident young lady to spend time with. She realized that once she let her "real" self shine through, others took notice.

Good for David! He realized that sometimes less is more. Sometimes an honest, simple, and sincere compliment goes a long way. It shows approval and admiration for people, or for their accomplishments. It is specific and truthful. Learning how to give and accept compliments are important relationship-building skills. When David gave that wonderful compliment to Tamika, he made sure that the compliment focused on her personality and ability, not her body parts. She was so tired of hearing flattery, which is insincere praise that is used for someone's own benefit, that she almost wrote David off. Now, Tamika not only enjoys receiving compliments from David, she loves giving him compliments for the smallest things he does. Giving sincere compliments that recognize a person's talents is a sure way to get a relationship started in the right direction.

RELATIONSHIP SKILL — GIVING COMPLIMENTS

1. Look at the person you are complimenting
    David looked directly at Tamika before speaking.

2.   Speak with a clear, enthusiastic voice

He eagerly approached Tamika and introduced himself right away!

3.   Praise the person's activity or project specifically; Tell him or her exactly what you like about it

David was very clear and concise about what he was praising Tamika for. He complimented her for how she ran her session. He specifically mentioned that she motivated and engaged her students.

4.   Give the other person time to respond to your compliment

After delivering his compliment, David paused and let Tamika respond to it. Nice job!

Characteristics of Language Cons

Language is powerful. It can build relationships or tear them down. How can you tell if someone is sincere in what he says – or if he's just trying to fool you into doing something you'll regret later?

Groomers and players use words like a weapon; there are elements that set their language apart from the norm. You can use this list to analyze the language of a potential groomer.

▽ Trying to convince the target that sex and love are the same thing – that sexual activity is the only way to prove love

▽ Specific, graphic, and even offensive sexual references

▽ **Coercive properties** – using words that threaten or intimidate

▽ **Possessiveness** – treating and talking about the target like an object that is owned

▽ **Repetitiveness** – constantly using the same words to gain the target's trust

▽ References to sexual behavior as a "duty" or "responsibility"

▽ References to sexual behavior as the ultimate proof of loyalty or maturity

▽ **Control** – using words that reinforce the groomer's position as "the boss"

Even when a target tries to end the relationship, the groomer will continue to use language cons. He certainly isn't going to take the blame or admit that any type of harmful relationship ever existed. He definitely isn't going to confess that he did anything wrong. He may lie or make threats, or try to convince others that the target is crazy. Sometimes, the groomer will say that the target made everything up: *"She's always wanted me, but since I didn't pay any attention to her, she just says things to get back at me."*

It can be very difficult for a target to find the best way to stop the abuse. When targets feel powerless and afraid, they are at a loss for what to do. Some targets don't make good choices; they try to solve the problem by running away, hurting themselves, getting further involved with alcohol and drugs, or even attempting suicide. Targets who tell

source: dictionary.com

com-pli-ment *noun*
1. an expression of praise, commendation, or admiration
2. a formal act or expression of civility, respect, or regard
3. compliments, a courteous greeting; good wishes; regards

checklist

Responding to Language Cons

Some people call language cons "lines." Lines or language cons are thinly veiled come-on statements or outright lies used to seduce or coerce someone into sexual activity. To remember what a line really is, just remove the "n" – and you'll see the lie.

When responding to language cons, it's important to:

Remember that language cons are used to trick, manipulate, and deceive.

People who use language cons are selfish and untrustworthy.

Pay close attention to a person's behaviors as well as his or her words.

The old saying, "A picture is worth a thousand words," applies here. Observe how a person treats others, and listen to what he or she says to others about dating, relationships, and sex. All of these can be important indicators of an emotional groomer's hidden intentions.

Learn and practice good social skills.

Developing good communication and refusal skills can help you resist giving in to threats or coercion. Build strong relationships with trustworthy adults you can go to for advice.

Don't waste time blaming yourself.

There are no excuses for using another person, especially in sexual ways. People who use language cons really only want to please themselves, not others. Sexual con artists need to bear the responsibility for their words and actions. If you become a target, focus on doing things to get better rather than blaming yourself.

Be as persistent in your refusal as the person who uses language cons.

He or she will use many different angles and keep trying to manipulate you. You have to be just as persistent and not give in.

Create and maintain healthy same-gender friendships.

Find good friends of the same gender who have your best interests at heart. These kinds of friends can "watch your back" and help you hear and see what you may not want to notice about someone else. In other words, friends can help each other unmask a sexual con artist.

Say Whaaat?

"I can live for two months on a good compliment."
— MARK TWAIN

someone who can help, like a trusted adult or older friend, stand the best chance of getting out of the abusive situation. Many targets turn to teachers or counselors for advice.

The target should realize that the groomer will be just as manipulative trying to get out of the relationship as he was getting into it. Sometimes, other people won't believe what the target says at first. This is partly because the groomer used language cons with them, too. Through manipulation, he has persuaded other people to believe him. However, if the target has the courage to tell the truth, and not give up, she is on the road to recovery.

WHat to Say

Saying "no" to someone is difficult, especially if that person is skilled at using language cons.

Having some idea of how you would respond can help you avoid the verbal traps set by someone who wants to convince you to have sex. You may want to use one of the following statements to help you stay in control when responding to a line.

"You don't really want me; you want sex."

"I'm not ready for sex. Don't try to push me into doing it."

"If you really care for me, you'll understand."

"Love is not sex; love is a commitment to make each other better."

"Real love isn't over in just a few minutes."

"You don't own my body. And I'm certainly not renting it out."

"Love is a two-way street. You only want it one-way: your way."

"I respect myself. Why can't you?"

"My brain's between my ears, not my legs."

"I want you to love me, not my body."

"I want real love, not an imitation."

"I have too much to lose."

"It's not worth it."

"Love is based on friendship, and you don't hurt friends."

"I want to be respected, not dejected."

"What part of 'no' don't you understand?"

"I know you don't understand, but I want you to respect my feelings."

"I care enough about you to do what's best for both of us."

"It's not right. I hope you understand."

"When I said 'no,' I meant it."

The Wired World

Make sure you are sincere and thoughtful when you give compliments to others. Sometimes without thinking, we may give an inappropriate compliment to someone online, Facebook, Twitter, Skype, etc. Remember, if we say things that are inappropriate, it's hard to take it back. Remember, too, that when you can't see someone's immediate reaction, you might say something hurtful or offensive without even realizing it!

Always remember to use the steps to the skill of "Giving Compliments" when you want to make your friends feel special. That way you will not need to follow it up with an additional skill of "Making an Apology!"

DANGER SIGNS

"I think I'm in love! I always feel the need to text my boyfriend constantly and just always think about him and depend my happiness on him. He texts me back. I know he loves me because he tells me that I'm pretty and mature. He said the other girls he dated are not mature because they did not want to have sex with him. He is always telling me nice things and it makes me feel good.

He told me that I belong to him and no one else. He said he cannot wait until we turn 16 so we can spend the night together. My friends are jealous because their boyfriends do not say nice things to them. I feel so special and lucky. I'm just really in love with him and feel that my happiness depends on him. I guess I'm insecure about myself."

 This girl definitely is being played. Her "boyfriend" is treating her like an object by telling her she "belongs to him and no one else." She admits that her happiness depends on him – that makes him (not her!) the boss of her life.

Saying 'No'

A 16-year-old girl wrote this letter to a 14-year-old boy who was frequently writing her notes. Notice the various ways in which she said "no."

"Hello. I am going to be very blunt and honest with you. NO. I do not like you at all and I have no interest in getting to know you whatsoever. First of all, you are younger than me and I am looking for different qualities in a guy than what you have. No, there's nothing wrong with you, but I want someone different and maturity is a main quality. Please quit writing me notes. No, I'm not going to give you a chance. Yes, you are wasting your time. Sorry, but I'm a blunt person. Lay off. Sorry if I broke your heart. Very uninterested and sorry."

Whoa! This girl is doing him a favor. She isn't leading him on or buying into his flattery. By being this honest, she's freeing him up to find someone his own age who will appreciate him.

CHAPTER

4

TIP > Gifts

GiFts
Not GraFt (Bribery)

Greg and Karon met two months ago at a high school football game during half-time. They bumped into each other at the concession stand. After a few awkward moments of exchanging greetings, they realized they were in the same chemistry class. Greg walked Karon back to her seat and told her that he looked forward to seeing her in class. She smiled and thought, "Man, he is so nice."

Monday afternoon, Greg walked into his sixth period chemistry class and saw Karon smiling as he entered the door. She gestured for him to sit next to her. He immediately walked over and did so. Karon reached in her purse and pulled out a nice blue box that she had decorated. She gave it to Greg and asked him to take it because he had been so nice to her at the game. Looking a little puzzled, Greg reluctantly took the box and discovered she had given him an expensive watch. He tried to return it to her, but she was not having any of it!

The next day, Karon approached Greg in the hallway and asked if he would go to the movies with her this weekend. As he was about to respond, she interrupted him and said, "I know you will go because I gave you that nice watch. I spent my hard-earned savings on it and there are more gifts for you if you are good to me!"

Greg's head was now spinning. "How did I get myself into this situation?" Greg immediately told Karon he would be returning the watch to her tomorrow. He realized she was using gifts to bribe her way into a relationship. He said, "That's too bad, because I really liked you Karon. And I would have gone out with you anyway. I did not need a watch in order to say yes. What I really wanted was just to spend some time getting to know you." Greg realized that he had gotten to know more about her than he ever wanted to.

The next day Greg returned the watch to Karon. He decided that from now on, he would greet her and then keep walking. Karon learned the hard way that you cannot use gifts as a way to bribe yourself into a meaningful relationship.

Karon did not realize that Greg was attracted to her at the football game because of her warm smile and pleasant conversation. She did not understand Greg only wanted the "gift" of her time and attention. Gifts should be given freely and without expecting anything in return. Karon now knows that an expensive watch was not an appropriate gift to give to someone she had just met. And using any gift as a bribe never results in a lasting, meaningful relationship.

Here are some tips to remember about gift-giving for an unofficial relationship:

⚡ You need a gift that says "I like you" but not "I want to meet your parents tomorrow."

Examples:

In the beginning – Lunch/dinner or favorite book

Later in the relationship – Nice dinner, flowers, inexpensive jewelry

⚡ **Rule number 1:** don't roll out the red carpet. Why? Well, you did just start dating and you want to save a little magic for later, if/when things get more serious. Plus, it may freak them out if you give them a present that most people save for their tenth wedding anniversary. Adapted from "Modern Manners Guy."

⚡ **Rule number 2:** also remember that small things like hand-written notes, cards, nice compliments, and attention go a long way!

RELATIONSHIP SKILL — CHOOSiNg Appropriate GiFtS

1. **Think about the type of relationship that you have with the person**

   Karon should have considered the fact that she did not know Greg at all. Maybe a "gift" of spending time to get to know each other would have been more appropriate.

2. **Determine the purpose of the gift**

   If Karon wanted to get to know Greg better, spending time together would be a nice and appropriate way to let him know that. It is obvious that Karon had another purpose in mind – bribery.

3. **Choose a gift that both you and the recipient will be comfortable with**

   This is important because Karon should have realized that an expensive gift was not appropriate at this early stage of the friendship. Greg would have probably felt more comfortable with a compliment, note, or a friendly gesture. Buying a gift for someone you recently started to get to know is tough. You don't want to freak them out by getting something too expensive. Simple is always better.

4. **Give the other person the gift, with no strings attached**

   Give your gift and only expect a thank-you in return. If you expect anything more than that, you have already attached "strings" to your gift.

Bribery

Bribery is "giving to get." The groomer may give material things to his target, but these "gifts" always have a string attached. In healthy relationships, giving gifts can be a normal sign of friendship or love. In an unhealthy relationship, a groomer gives "gifts" in order to bribe or manipulate the target. The target may think that something, usually some sort of sexual behavior, must be done to "pay back" the groomer so that the attention and gifts will continue.

Sometimes, the bribe that convinces a target to stay with a groomer may be the promise of marriage or of always being together. Female groomers will often use the promise of sex as a bribe to get and keep a guy in a relationship. In some relationships, the bribes are alcohol or drugs. This is an old trick used by pimps with their prostitutes: Get them addicted to a substance and they will do whatever the pimp wants.

Say Whaaat?

"If I could do it, I'd buy you everything you wanted. Remember that sweater at the mall. That would look so good on you baby. Someday I'll buy it or steal it if I have to. You mean the world to me and I want to show you how much. You just keep being good to me, you'll see."

Bribery can sometimes be very blatant and very destructive. A 16-year-old girl told her teacher: "When I was 13, my boyfriend, who was 19, took me to the fair. He won one of those big stuffed teddy bears. When we got home he told me he'd give me the bear if I had sex with him. How come when he was on top of me, I started crying?" The teacher responded, "You cried because he was taking something precious from you that you weren't ready to give. That's where the tears came from." It's obvious that this groomer used bribery to get what he wanted. He gave a 13-year-old girl a toy in order to get sex from her.

Tips For Appropriate Gift Giving

1. Don't buy anything too expensive.

    For a new relationship, it's best not to spend more than $10 to $15, if anything at all. Anything over that price might make your new guy/girlfriend feel like you're taking the relationship too seriously, too fast. Plus, if your partner has gotten you something less lavish, it will make for an awkward situation.

2. **Stay away from gifts that are too small/simple.**

On the other end of the spectrum, don't get a gift that is too small. While you don't want to overspend, you also don't want the gift to be something too generic. The key is to show that you've enjoyed the time you've spent so far, have listened and learned a bit about them and would like to continue down that road.

3. **Stay away from gifts that are too personal.**

It's not a good idea to give something that injects yourself into your new guy/girlfriend's life too fast. You have to let the other person open up their life to you at their own pace. Getting too intense, too quickly, is a sure-fire way to creep her/him out.

4. **Avoid gifts that can send the wrong message.**

This is straightforward enough. If you can imagine your new guy/girlfriend reading too much into something or interpreting the meaning of an item in a different way than you intended, leave it at the store and walk away.

The Wired World

Gift giving is difficult in the Wired World. Compliments may be the best gift you can give a friend in the wired world. Just make sure your words are sincere. Also, do not accept gifts from people you do not know or feel comfortable with online. Always use caution.

"*I love my boyfriend with all my heart; he means the world to me. We have been together for about five months now. We fight quite a bit, but it never makes either one of us love each other any less. Recently, I discovered him flirting and making sexual comments to another girl from his church. Feeling as if I had no other option, I broke up with him. Then he started buying me gifts and saying that he did not know what he would do if I left him.*

He seems to buy me things whenever we have problems. I love him so I can't stay mad at him. Last week he bought me a pretty ring. I needed money for gas – and yes, he paid for it. He told me that I should not get upset with him because those other girls are not important like me.

My mom thinks our relationship is 'unhealthy' and 'he might bring me down if I continue to date him.' Do you think this is true? On the other hand, I think it should be my choice and I will figure things out sooner or later. I know that I am a very strong person and if things get too bad I will leave him even though I am so in love. How can I tell my mom he is a good guy and that she needs to continue letting me and him see each other? Right now, breaking up with him over this is not an option."

Whoa! This girl's boyfriend is bribing her. He's fooling around and covering it up later by spending money on her. If she's as important to him as he claims she is, he'll change his behavior – not "buy" her affection.

45

CHAPTER 5

 Similarities

SiMiLaritieS
Not status

Janelle and Samantha are best friends.
They are both 17 years old. Samantha has always dated guys 4 to 5 years older than her because she felt like the guys her age were too young and immature. She would often tell Janelle that she needs to start dating older men and stop fooling around with young losers.

Janelle and her boyfriend, Aaron, are the same age. They have been dating for about a year and have lots of friends and activities in common. They are often seen with groups of friends going to sporting events and school dances. Janelle and Aaron would decide on what activities they would do together. They also take time to hang out as a couple at their favorite coffee house.

Last weekend, Janelle invited Samantha and her current boy-friend, Martin, to go to a movie with her and Aaron. Samantha said, "You know that Martin will not go for that idea. He loves me so much and wants me to spend time with him. He said that he doesn't like to hang out with groups of people. I better check my phone because he will be contacting me soon to go to the tattoo shop. We are getting tattoos today."

It seemed strange that Samantha was getting a tattoo since she had previously told Janelle that she hated them. When Janelle pressed her about the tattoo, Samantha admitted that she still did not like them, but did not want Martin to get mad. Janelle tried to convince Samantha to back off seeing Martin so exclusively because he seemed very possessive and controlling. She told Samantha that he seemed like he was not interested in getting to know her – he was more interested in controlling her. Janelle tried to convince Samantha that she and Martin had nothing in common.

Janelle realized her friendship with Samantha was crumbling. She told Samantha that she will always be there for her, but being around her right now was becoming too painful. She also realized that she does not ever want to be in an unhealthy relationship where her boyfriend is much older and doesn't fit in with her friends and wants to control her. She knows that good relationships have equal partners – people of about the same age and the same place in life.

Several months passed, and then one evening Samantha called Janelle after dinner. Samantha could hardly speak audibly through her tears. She asked Janelle to forgive her for abandoning their friendship. She said she realized that Martin was no good for her and they had nothing in common. She was tired of being fearful of him. She wanted to hang out with her best friend again and not with someone who was too abusive and controlling.

source: dictionary.com

sim·i·lar *adjective*
1. having a likeness or resemblance, especially in a
   general way

The best relationships are between two people who have some similarities – such as the same values and level of life experience. Samantha started off liking the status she had from dating older guys. She believed "getting" an older guy meant she was more mature or important than Janelle.

In reality, status is a dangerous dating game to play. Someone who's older and more experienced may be on a different path. If dating partners are unequal in experience, one can easily control the other. For example, Martin doesn't want to hang out with Samantha's friends – he's so much older and doesn't "fit in" to her life very well. Martin should stick to dating women in his own age group, who are as experienced as he is and more likely to share some of his interests.

The truth of the matter is that when someone much older wants to "date" a girl or guy still in high school, it's smart to question that person's motives. Odds are the older person can't get what he/she wants from someone his/her own age and finds that a younger person who is dazzled by status is much easier to manipulate.

In Samantha's case, she woke up and realized Martin was no good for her – he was using her and cutting her off from her friends. The status she's received (or thought she was getting) from having an older boyfriend resulted in an unhealthy, unequal relationship, and she's ready to get back to her life. She wants to have a relationship like Janelle and Aaron have, based on friends and activities in common.

Say Whaaat?

"The key is to get to know people and trust them to be who they are. Instead, we trust people to be who we want them to be – and when they're not, we cry." – SAMUEL JOHNSON

RELATIONSHIP SKILL
Making New Friends

1. **Share some of your interests and hobbies**

    Janelle and Aaron enjoyed sharing friends, hobbies, and interests with each other. They had lots of things in common. On the other hand, Samantha and Martin seemed to have very little in common. Martin was so much older, and his privileges (having his own place) and life circumstances were so different. It was the set-up for Martin to use his status as an older guy to control and manipulate Samantha.

2. **Listen to the other person's areas of interest**

    Martin forced his interests on Samantha without regards to her feelings. Seems as though he did not care whether or not she liked tattoos, he just wanted her to get one because it served his interest. He never asked her opinion. Healthy friendships and/or dating relationships require both parties to listen to each other's interest. Janelle and Aaron, on the other hand, really listened to each other and respected each other's wishes.

3. **Plan appropriate activities with permission**

    Janelle and Aaron planned and mutually decided which activities they would participate in. They made sure that any activities planned would be appropriate and comfortable for both of them. They always sought permission and were in agreement with each other. Seeking permission has helped them to maintain a healthy and caring relationship.

What you want from a relationship in the early months of dating may be quite different from what you want after you have been together for some time. Anticipate that both you and your partner will change over time. Feelings of love and passion change with time, as well. Respecting and valuing these changes is healthy. Love literally changes brain chemistry for the first months of a relationship. For both physiological and emotional reasons, an established relationship will have a more complex and often richer type of passion than a new relationship.

It is difficult, but healthy, to accept there are some things about our friends that will not change over time, no matter how much we want them to. Unfortunately, there is often an expectation that our friends will change only in the ways we want. We may also hold the unrealistic expectation that our friends will never change from the way he or she is now.

In healthy relationships, there is respect for each person's right to have her/his own feelings, friends, activities, and opinions. It is unrealistic to expect or demand that he or she have the same priorities, goals, and interests as you.

The Wired World

Your Wired World can be a dangerous place, indeed, for finding dating partners who share your interests and who are compatible age-wise. People make up all kinds of things about themselves so they can attract someone online. They inflate their "status" in terms of appearance, money, possessions, activities, etc., to get people interested.

DATING!

You need to know someone face-to-face before you communicate online; otherwise, you're likely to get lured in by false information.

On the other hand, some people go online to brag about their relationships. They are very quick to change their relationship status from "Single" to "In a Relationship." They think that kind of status change makes them more important. Really, all they're doing is inviting everyone to get involved in their personal business. Then, when things end (as they often do – and badly, too!) they're left having to explain the situation.

DANGER SIGNS

When the age gap is more than a year or two (for high school students) the door is open for one person to control and even abuse another. A person who is out of school and a legal adult has access to all sorts of activities that a high school person does not. It's easy to be fooled by someone who seems so mature and who appears to be in charge.

Don't Know What To Call It...

"There is this older man. He is about 26 and I am 17 years old. I see him every summer when I visit my grandma in Vermont. He liked to rub my back and my stomach and my arms and my legs and he liked to play with my hair. He never touched my privates or anything, but he loved to have me sit on his lap – whether I wanted to or not. I didn't go once and he just kept insisting, so I went. He said he wanted to wash my hair and was obsessed with it. He liked to lay down with me, and once when I was sleeping, he massaged my feet.

I think we kissed on the lips once, and he was always telling me that he loved me. Also, he had a lot of pictures of kids on his camera and phone. They were fully dressed or in swim suits. A lot of his kid friends had swim meets and he'd take pictures. I think he just cared about them all, but not in a bad way. I don't know.

I think the pictures were innocent. I don't know what to think because there are a lot of people who think he is dangerous, or could be. I really don't think I was molested, but I am not entirely sure and I don't know what to call this. Please help."

 This young woman is being victimized by a skilled groomer. He lured her in with the status of being older and more "mature" and now is using her. If you or a friend is being pursued by an adult, make sure to tell your parents or another adult you trust. This type of relationship never is healthy or safe.

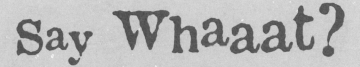

Say Whaaat?

"A great relationship is about two things, first, find out the similarities, second, respect the differences."

– ANONYMOUS

CHAPTER 6

TIP Generosity

GeNerosity
Not JeaLousy
aNd PossessiveNess

Raj and Mala have been dating for six months. Raj has been asking Mala to invite him over to her house to meet her family. Each time he asks, Mala declines. She has hesitated to have any friends come over because she has felt as though her family overlooks her and spends more time with her friends than with her. She has become very possessive and even a little jealous of her friends and family. Mala believed that once her family met Raj, she would be forgotten by both her family and Raj – just like the last time she brought someone home.

As Mala reflected on her feelings, she recognized that the "green-eyed monster" of jealousy was rearing up its head – again, trying to take control of her. She remembered that her jealous and possessive feelings destroyed her last relationship when she got into a heated argument with her former boyfriend about her family spending more time with him than with her. Therefore, Mala decided it was time for a change, so she invited Raj to come to her house to meet her family. She did not want to see this relationship end.

Say Whaaat?

"My wife's jealousy is getting ridiculous.
The other day she looked at my calendar and
wanted to know who May was."

— RODNEY DANGERFIELD

Raj came over for dinner the following weekend. He arrived at the door with beautiful fresh flowers for Mala. She was both excited and surprised because she seldom received gifts from her dates. He met her younger brother Chahel, younger sister Oja, and her parents. He noticed that her brother was finishing up his math homework before dinner. He asked him if he liked math. Chahel said math was his least favorite subject. Raj informed Chahel that he was a math tutor at his school and would be happy to tutor him if he would like. Chahel turned to ask Mala if that would be okay. She was now thinking – here we go again! Then she thought that she was going to make an effort to include Raj in activities with her family.

Coincidentally, the tutoring arrangement was beneficial to her also because it meant she would not be the only one helping Chahel with his homework. They agreed to spend time together helping him with his math. Mala realized that she liked sharing her attention with Raj to help her brother. She was now spending quality time with both of them. There was no need for any competition or jealousy.

Mala overheard a conversation between her mom and dad after dinner. Her dad said, "I know that we are always asking Mala to help with tutoring and other things for the family. We depend on her so much because she is so reliable. I hope that she doesn't feel that we are taking her for granted. We should let Mala know how important she is to us. Let's put all plans aside and spend time with her this weekend." Mala had no idea her father felt that way about her. She now sees how her possessive feelings were deceiving her.

Raj also invited Mala to go to a baseball game with his family the following weekend. Raj's family loved Mala. They thought she was a wonderful young lady and fun to be around. By sharing both attention and time with others, Mala realized she had learned a lot about others and herself. She now sees her relationship with Raj is on a healthy track, and there is no need to feel jealous. He in turn finds her generosity extremely attractive.

Mala's learning some tough lessons about jealousy and possessiveness. What is jealousy, anyway? According to Webster's dictionary, jealousy is described as "the state of being jealous." In order to unravel the circular reasoning we must discover what jealous means. Jealous is a resentful envy of someone's success, achievements, advantages, etc.

Envy and jealousy are closely related, however, a connotation difference exists. To quote Webster, "Envy denotes a longing to possess something awarded to or achieved by another. . ." Jealousy refers to "anguish caused by fear of losing someone or something to a rival."

As you may have gathered from the above explanations, jealousy can be unhealthy or healthy, depending on your motivation. Unhealthy jealousy stems from fear, insecurity, deception, or covetousness. When you feel yourself acting out in jealousy, you need to examine the reason why you feel jealous.

Does a threat truly exist or is your perception off base?

But everyone feels jealous some time or another, right? True! The key to healthy relationships lies in learning how to handle jealousy, and all our other feelings, appropriately. The next time you feel the angst of jealousy creep into your chest, stop, think, and discern the source of jealousy. Once you discover why you are jealous, you need to deal with the issue.

One method of handling emotions appropriately is to **name, claim** and **tame** your feelings.

Name Spend some time figuring out what it is you are feeling. Often we just react to negative or difficult feelings without really being aware of the actual emotion. It is helpful to name your feeling, so that you can move beyond it.

Claim To claim your feeling means to own it. "I feel jealous" is different from "You make me so jealous." Using "I" language helps you to recognize the feeling as your own, rather than blaming it on others.

Tame To tame a feeling means to find a way to express it appropriately, without hurting yourself or someone else. Usually this means finding a trusted adult or wise friend who will help you name and claim your feelings, encourage you to find ways to express feelings appropriately (like writing in a journal, talking it out, crying, counseling, etc.) and, finally, who will support you in accepting and letting go of the emotion. Taming ultimately involves recognizing and accepting what you can and cannot control in life. It's not an easy process, but it will help you grow and enjoy happier and healthier relationships.

One fact you need to know about jealousy is that it usually stems from insecurity. While you may feel like you're mad at your partner because of the way he's talking to another woman, the reality is that the feeling probably comes from your insecurities. You're not really upset at how he's acting, but rather are just being reminded of your own insecurities in the relationship – that he might cheat on you or leave you for someone else.

Mala discovered that sharing and generosity in the long run make her happier than hoarding everyone's time and attention all for herself. When she's not busy making sure she gets her fair share of the limelight, she can relax and enjoy everything happening around her. The other people in her life are more likely to want to spend time around her, too!

RELATIONSHIP SKILL   Sharing Attention With Others

1.   Calmly share your attention with another person

Mala initially did not want to share her time or attention with anybody. She hoarded relationships with her possessiveness.

2.   Avoid distracting behaviors such as whining, laughing loudly, or complaining

Mala would complain to her family whenever she felt like they were spending too much time with her friends. She would also argue with her friends because she felt they focused too much time on her family.

3.   Include others in activities

Mala finally invited Raj over to dinner. In addition, she agreed to have him co-tutor her brother with her.

Finally, Raj reciprocated by inviting her to a baseball game with his family. By sharing her attention with others, Mala realized that in the past she had been missing out on many positive experiences.

The Wired World

How do you practice generosity in the Wired World? You start by understanding and accepting that you don't "own" the people you date – they have a right to relationships, conversations and activities that don't revolve around you. If you're generous and kind with those you date, you don't constantly check up on them online, or feel like you always have to comment online whenever they post something or reply to someone else. You allow space.

DANGER SIGNS

When possessiveness and jealousy take over, it's only a matter of time (and usually not too much time!) before a relationship crashes and burns.

Don't Want Our Relationship Messed Up

"So my boyfriend's off for Spring Break without me. We've been seeing each other for about 3 ½ months and he hasn't done anything to make me distrust him or feel insecure, but we all know what goes down during Spring Break. He said he was going home to visit his family but who knows what might happen.

I can't help but worry that he's going to cheat on me. I don't want him to talk to any of those tramps down there. I know I'm obsessing about this but hey – I can't help it! I get really upset whenever he talks to a pretty girl. I wonder if he wants to leave me like my last boyfriend did! I call him about six times a day to see what he's doing. These jealous thoughts have been in my mind for some time now and I don't know how to deal with it! I really don't want our relationship to get messed up and all this worrying is causing me stress and anxiety."

 This young woman is consumed with jealousy. She's treating her boyfriend like a possession she owns, not like a person who has a right to his own thoughts, feelings, and friendships.

In the meantime, she's causing herself a great deal of trouble. By spending all of her time worrying about where her boyfriend is and what he's doing, she's missing out on her own interests, friendships, and family. When the relationship ends (and it's likely that will happen sooner rather than later) she'll be left trying to put her life back together.

She needs to Name, Claim, and Tame the green-eyed monster called Jealousy. It's time for her to talk with an adult she trusts, and ask for help. She needs to "get a life" apart from her boyfriend, and learn to give him some space. That way, she can enjoy the relationship (and so can he!) without letting it take over her life.

Say Whaaat?

"The **jealous are troublesome** to others, but a torment to themselves."
— WILLIAM PENN

CHAPTER

7

TIP Self-Assurance

SeLF-ASSUraNce
Not SeLF-DouBt (INSecUrity)

Maria and Arturo live down the street from each other. They attend the same high school. Occasionally, Arturo would greet Maria as she jogged down the street to the park. As he returned from the store one Saturday morning, he noticed Maria jogging past his house. He asked her if she would mind if he jogged with her. She told him she didn't mind, but he would have to keep pace with her because she was conditioning for a 5k race for charity.

As they jogged, Arturo became very interested in what she was trying to accomplish. He asked her how long she had been racing for charity and why. She mentioned that her sister has Multiple Sclerosis and this was her way of helping to find a cure. Immediately, Arturo knew that she was special. Not only was she very beautiful on the outside, but her beauty shone even brighter from within. He told Maria that he was impressed with her kind and selfless act. He asked if he could support her cause by running the race with her. She looked at him, smiled, and said, "Absolutely, the more the merrier!"

Arturo soon realized that running with Maria was not only a healthy activity; it was also a great way to get to know her better! Maria learned that Arturo loved to shoot hoops at the neighborhood community center. She dropped by one Saturday to watch him play ball with his friends. Afterwards, she complimented him on scoring a couple 3-pointers. "Wow, I had no idea you had game. That was awesome!" she said.

Arturo and Maria learned to appreciate each other's talents and accomplishments. There was no competition, only respect. After one month of "hanging out," Arturo asked Maria to a movie. They have been dating ever since!

In healthy relationships, people feel increased self-confidence when their dating partners encourage and support their interests and talents. Arturo became more attracted to Maria because of the charitable activities she was involved in. She, in turn, developed an interest in him because of his support and encouragement to her. People in healthy relationships realize that it is more important to invest in their partners, rather than compete, or become jealous or insecure about what they are trying to accomplish.

Sometimes insecurity creeps into relationships. Like jealousy, insecurity is a normal human emotion. In some cases, it's even appropriate to feel somewhat insecure. That is why it becomes very important for couples to have separate activities to be involved in; this provides an opportunity for them to become self-confident in their own abilities. It is also important for them to engage in some activities together. This provides an opportunity to really get to know each other by spending time together.

Maria and Arturo are learning that a healthy relationship requires sharing, giving compliments, supporting each other, and a sense of self-confidence. They're also learning that put downs, mean teasing, and unkind words have no place in a healthy relationship.

MaKing Positive Statements about Others

1. Try to notice or find out positive things or events about others

   Arturo paid special attention to the things that Maria was involved in. He noticed that she spent many hours jogging through the neighborhood. He showed interest by finding out what she was trying to accomplish.

2. Use clear, enthusiastic tone of voice

   When Arturo learned about Maria's upcoming event, he became excited and asked if he could run the race with her.

Say Whaaat?

"Power is of two kinds. One is obtained by the fear of punishment and the other by acts of love. Power based on love is a thousand times more effective and permanent than the one derived from fear of punishment."
— MAHATMA GANDHI

> source: dictionary.com
>
> **in·se·cu·ri·ty** *noun*
> 1. lack of confidence or assurance; self-doubt
> 2. the quality or state of being insecure; instability
> 3. something insecure

3. **Praise a specific trait or ability of the other person, or congratulate him or her on a recent accomplishment**

    He immediately told Maria how impressed he was for the decision to volunteer her time for a special cause. Maria was also complimentary to Arturo for his great basketball skills.

4. **Don't say anything that would invalidate your compliment**

    They kept all compliments positive and on point.

The Wired World

When using social media and other forms of wired technology, remember to put some thought into your statements to your friends. Keep it positive at all times – don't give in to the temptation to criticize or put your boyfriend or girlfriend down (either in your words to them or when "talking" about them with others).

Sometimes sarcastic remarks or dark humor do not translate well in the Wired World. You may think that you are giving your friend a compliment by saying, "Glad to see that you bought some new jeans. Those other ones did not look good on you." Those types of comments invalidate the compliment that you were trying to make. Concentrate on your friend's ability or good qualities. Remember, what you "say" online or text takes on a life of its own – make sure your words build up instead of tear down.

✓ checklist

Tips to Building
Self-confidence in Dating

Use the past as a guide and build off of it

Don't worry over what could've been or what should've been. It will only bring you down. Instead, gather all the information you've learned from your past relationships. Repeat what has worked well and avoid making mistakes a second time.

Get out of your Comfort Zone

Gathering new, challenging experiences and accomplishments under your belt will make you more confident. And greater trust in yourself leads to greater self-confidence, which will positively affect how you approach dating.

Be proud of what you have accomplished

If you are able to recognize things you have done that you are proud of it will strengthen your core self-respect and help build true inner-confidence.

✦ ✦ ✦ ✦ ✦ ✦ ✦ ✦ ✦ ✦ ✦

Like what you see in the mirror

When you look good, it's more likely that you'll feel good about yourself. Take a good look in the mirror and evaluate yourself and your look. What could you update, and how could you improve your personal style?

Go Easy on Yourself

Relax and have fun on dates. Don't pressure yourself with expectations. That way you'll never be disappointed, only pleasantly surprised. Don't let negative experiences get you down. Take your time, enjoy and embrace the opportunity you have to sample meeting and getting to know different types of people, experience personal growth, and accumulate new experiences.

DANGER SIGNS

When put downs and threats of self-harm undermine you (Insecurity)

Like jealousy, insecurity is a normal human emotion. In some cases, it's even appropriate to feel somewhat insecure (if you don't know anything about science, for example, and you're in a room full of nuclear physicists, you're likely to feel insecure). And, like jealousy, insecurity is harmful when it is used to manipulate someone else.

Dating partners can use insecurity in two ways. One way is to act insecure and ask for constant reassurance of a girl/boyfriend's love and loyalty. The girl/boyfriend then is expected to take care of this insecurity by endless verbal and physical displays of attention. The insecure dating partner also may want pity and sympathy – someone to feel sorry for her/him.

"I guess it's no big deal. I just don't think I'm really your type or good enough for you. I'm screwing too many things up. I'm not worth it. So let me know if you want to stop our relationship. I'll try to understand. I probably deserve it anyway. The way I treat you, I'm not doing it the way I'm supposed to. I guess I was wrong. I'm sorry for treating you the way I did."

Whoa! When this form of insecurity gets truly dangerous, the insecure dating partner may say something like, "I'll kill myself if you leave me!" Use great caution if you hear this statement. It may just be an idle threat, a ploy used to get you to stay in the relationship. But we never know for sure what someone else's true intentions are. If you ever hear someone threatening suicide or to hurt you or someone else, you must tell an adult – a parent, a teacher, a counselor, a police officer, or a pastor. You could also call the Boys Town Hotline® at 800-448-3000.

It is never your obligation to stay in a relationship with a person who is threatening to hurt him or herself, but it is your obligation to tell an adult who can help. Threats of self-harm can sometimes turn into harm acted out against others. Criminal justice advocate Laura Delgado says it this way, "A threat of suicide is exactly the same as a threat of homicide... It says that 'I don't have anything to lose.'"

Say Whaaat?

"Friends can help each other.
A true friend is someone who lets you have total
freedom to be yourself – and especially to feel.
Or, not feel. Whatever you happen to be feeling at
the moment is fine with them. That's what real love
amounts to – letting a person be what he really is."

– JIM MORRISON

When someone attempts to magnify their girl/
boyfriend's insecurities or create new insecurities

*"No one else will ever want you. I'm the only one who
is ever going to want you. You'd be stupid to pass up a guy
like me. I'm the man. Once I'm through with you, you'll
never want anybody else."*

This kind of manipulation is an attempt to control the
other person's thoughts and feelings. The game here is to
make someone feel so bad and so insecure that he/she will
stay in the unhealthy relationship and be reluctant to open
up to others.

The young woman who wrote this letter is a target for
both forms of insecurity. Her boyfriend keeps her endlessly
off-balance by both criticizing her and then threatening to
hurt himself.

source: thefreedictionary.com

self-as·sur·ance *noun*
1. confidence in the validity, value, etc.,
   of one's own ideas, opinions, etc.

70

I'M Scared oF Being Hurt

"Me and my boyfriend have been dating for eight months. He cheated on me more than once. He's always talking to other girls and said that I better be glad that I am dating him because no one else would want me. He tells me that I dress nicely, but I am too fat! He is always saying something good to me, and then he turns around and calls me names.

I tried to break up with him, but he tells me he will kill himself if I leave him. I love him and don't want to let him hurt himself. I know he loves me because he is still with me and says nice things to me most of the time. What do I do because I know he needs me?"

Whoa! He's emotionally abusing her – and things could get very dangerous very quickly. Her best strategy is to talk to an adult she trusts, and to get out of the relationship as soon and as safely as possible.

CHAPTER
8

TIP ▶ Accuracy

Accuracy
Not Accusation

Lynette has been dating her boyfriend Eric for two years now. When they first met, he took pride in being well-groomed. Eric would make sure he was clean-shaven and dressed appropriately for whatever the occasion might be. He worked out on a regular basis and enjoyed spending time with Lynette.

Recently, Eric has said he wants to ditch that preppy attire and look more 'normal' like his new friends. He now wears dirty cut-off shorts; his hair looks greasy and messy. He spends more time with his new friends, and often excludes Lynette.

Lynette's not sure how to tell Eric how she feels about his new grooming habits and aloofness. Normally she would "just tell it like it is," not caring about the other person's feelings. After watching her abusive parents fight on a regular basis, she realizes she wants to change the way she expresses her feelings to others. She recognizes she and Eric have invested time in their relationship and she believes it was worth trying to save. With that in mind, she decided to ask Eric to go with her to their favorite coffee shop to hang out. Maybe, she thought, this would be a good place to calmly express how she was feeling about the "new" Eric.

Lynette was very nervous when Eric walked through the door at the coffee shop. She smiled and greeted him with a hug. Lynette knew it was now or never to express how she really felt to Eric. She took two deep breaths and reflected on how she would want to be approached if she was the one on the receiving end. After making small talk, Lynette held Eric's hand and said she wanted to talk to him about an important issue. She calmly described how confused she had become with his new style of dress. She said she thought he had a great sense of style and wondered why he would want to change it. She also stated she missed spending time with him because he seemed to spend a lot of time with his new friends without including her, and she would like to get to know them, too.

She was careful not to argue or make accusations against him like her parents usually would do to each other. She simply stated her feelings to him, and then told him he was such a great person. "Please don't 'lose' yourself by trying to be like someone else. Those were the wonderful qualities that attracted me to you," she said.

With tears in his eyes, Eric acknowledged he had been trying to be different to fit in with everyone else. He just wanted to feel respected. He apologized to Lynette and stated he would never want to hurt their relationship. He hugged her, and then thanked her for expressing how she felt in a caring way. She told Eric how much she appreciated him, and how glad she was he listened to her and took her seriously.

Say Whaaat?

"When one person makes an accusation, check to be sure he himself is not the guilty one. Sometimes it is those whose case is weak who make the most clamour."

– PIERS ANTHONY

It can be scary to share your true feelings with someone you care about, particularly if it's about a sensitive subject. What if she/he gets angry? What if you get angry and say things you don't mean or just say the first thing that comes to your mind, without really thinking and choosing your words carefully? What if what you say makes things worse, not better?

In healthy relationships, partners don't fall back on accusations – they can say how they feel without blaming, cursing, or hurting the other person's feelings. They are able to take responsibility for their own thoughts and feelings, and are sensitive but honest. If you can't be honest, your relationship can't grow and ultimately will suffer.

Remember, the reason you take time to share your honest feelings is because you care about the other person. You care about your relationship, too, and want to help each other be the best you can be.

source: thefreedictionary.com

con·cern *noun*
1. A matter that relates to or affects one.
2. Regard for or interest in someone or something.
3. A troubled or anxious state of mind arising from solicitude or interest.

RELATIONSHIP SKILL — EXpreSSiNg FeeliNgS AppropriateLy

1. **Look at the person you're talking to and remain calm and relaxed**

   Lynette met Eric in a quiet place. She smiled and took two deep breaths to calm and relax herself before she ever said a word.

2. **Describe the feelings you're currently having**

   Lynette stated her feelings clearly.

3. **Take ownership of your feelings and avoid statements of blame**

   Lynette "took ownership" of her feelings; she didn't blame Eric, but merely stated her own thoughts and ideas about what was happening.

4. **Thank the person for listening**

   Lynette told Eric how much it meant to her that he would listen and take her seriously.

False allegations arise for the following reasons:

- ⚙ Sheer bitterness and envy against the success or person of the victim. The victim may also be vulnerable and he/she is defenseless.

- ⚙ The accuser is simply lacking in self-confidence.

- ⚙ The accuser and the victim are in a trusting position.

- ⚙ The victim may have offended the false accuser (via failed promises, via what the accuser sees as action or inaction, use or misuse of words, etc.) to the extent that the accuser decided to torment the victim. This could be a case of misunderstanding.

⚙ It's all about self-preservation and survival. The accuser is selfish or wants promotion, recognition and fame.

⚙ The victim being accused is not careful enough to know the nature of the accuser and so may divulge confidential information to the false accuser who will in turn twists words and the other person's good intentions.

⚙ The victim may be behaving in a way to suggest and/or give strength to the accuser to advance the true event beyond what actually happened.

⚙ The accuser may be acting at the orders or instruction of a third party that may be envious or bitter towards the victim. So the accuser is a "mule" or "puppet" in the hands of the real person.

Sometimes, out of jealousy or insecurity, people are overly suspicious that their dating partners are cheating on them or doing something they don't (or won't) approve

Say Whaaat?

"Love is like playing the piano. First you must learn to play by the rules, then you must forget the rules and play from your heart."

– ANONYMOUS

of or like. They create false or exaggerated accusations to frighten, threaten and ultimately control their boyfriends or girlfriends. For example, a guy might accuse his girlfriend of having sex with other guys or talking about him behind his back. Regardless of the specifics of the accusation, the real intent is to publicly intimidate and perhaps even humiliate the other person, thus maximizing the accuser's sense of control.

source: thefreedictionary.com

ac·cu·sa·tion *noun*
1. An act of accusing or the state of being accused.
2. A charge of wrongdoing that is made against a person or other party.

The Wired World

Remember playing the game "Telephone" when you were little? You started off with one phrase, but after whispering it to others, it came out at the end of the line as something completely different than when you started.

The same applies to expressing honest feelings in the Wired World. When you have something sensitive to discuss with your dating partner, the smart move is to talk face-to-face (like Lynette and Eric) after you've calmed down and thought seriously about what you really want to say. If you can't be in the same place at the same time, then make use of the phone and at least talk "voice-to-voice" – this cuts down on miscommunication and shows caring and respect.

My boyfriend and I have been together for 3 months. He asked me to prom and I found the perfect dress.

Now, it's just five days before the dance. Tonight, he sent me a text and said he doesn't really want to go out with me anymore and our prom date is off. I forwarded his text to all my friends and asked them what they think is going on. They all said he must be cheating on me. Then, I texted him back and said I can't believe he's doing this to me, and I bet he's cheating on me with the girl I always see hanging around his locker.

My heart is breaking! I don't know what I did wrong. I want to call him, but I don't know what to say!

This girl has every reason to be upset – "breaking up" with someone via text is cowardly at best, and certainly is hurtful. On the other hand, dragging all of her friends into it and making unfounded accusations isn't helping matters, either. Her best bet now is to talk through her hurt and disappointment with an adult she trusts, and then ask to talk with her boyfriend face-to-face to find out what's really happening. After she has all of the facts, she can decide what to do next.

CHAPTER

9

 Serenity

Serenity
Not Struggle (Anger)

Monique is a junior in high school. She and Anthony have been dating for several months. Last night she became very upset with Anthony because he gave Regina, a longtime friend of his, a ride to her job after school. When Anthony tried to explain that Regina's car was in the shop and that he was just doing her a favor, Monique became more and more agitated.

Monique confessed, "I get upset because my last boyfriend was spending time with me while hooking up with his old girl-friend. So when you say Regina is just a friend, it's hard for me to believe that. I don't want to get angry and upset. I guess I have issues with trusting people. My problem started awhile back when my parents sabotaged the trust that I had for them. They had me believing that I was their natural born daughter until I stumbled across some papers that revealed I was adopted. Can you believe it? All of this time I thought they were my real parents! I'm so tired of lies and I have a hard time controlling my emotions when someone lies to me. Wait, I know I may be projecting my feelings on you, and that's not cool."

Anthony paused for a moment. He thought about how much he enjoyed being around Monique every day. He looked at her and said, "Monique, I know I have not experienced what you have been going through. I don't want you to become angry or hurt because of situations you cannot control. I'm sorry your parents lied to you, but if we are going to have a meaningful relationship, we have got to learn how to deal with stressful situations and trust each other. I care about you and don't want to see you like this."

Monique apologized and said she will work on controlling her emotions by pausing, taking deep breaths, and addressing her feelings in a calm manner. She realized she wanted her relationship with Anthony to grow into something special and she was not going to let her emotions control her.

Everyone feels anger sometimes, but in healthy relationships the anger is never used to frighten or alienate the other person. Unfortunately, Monique had experienced some hurtful situations with her parents and former boyfriend in the past. She now has a hard time trusting anyone, including Anthony, her current boyfriend.

Monique's emotions were out of control. She imagined the worst in most situations. Her emotions were starting to affect her new relationship with Anthony. She expressed to Anthony why she was so distrustful and angry. She also apologized and promised to work on ways to conquer those ugly emotions. She has decided to "check herself, before she wrecks herself."

source: thefreedictionary.com

se·ren·i·ty *noun*
1. The state or quality of being serene.

Good for her to recognize that Anthony had nothing to do with her past experiences. He empathized with her and then expressed to her the importance of dealing with two issues – anger and trust – if they are going to have a healthy relationship. Monique knows she must end the drama and start out with a "clean slate" of trust and serenity in this new relationship.

Anthony showed great maturity by sharing his feelings in a calm way, and not letting Monique's behavior go on without addressing it. He did her a favor by pointing out what was happening.

Say Whaaat?

"God grant me the serenity to accept the things I cannot change, the courage to change the things I can, and the wisdom to know the difference."
— REINHOLD NIEBUHR

RELATIONSHIP SKILL — CONTROLLING EMOTIONS

1. **Learn what situations cause you to lose control or make you angry**

   Monique was very aware of what caused her to become angry. She held on to the disappointments from the past.

2. **Monitor the feelings you have in stressful situations**

   To Monique's credit, she quickly recognized that she was becoming stressed.

   She later developed coping strategies to address that stress.

3. **Instruct yourself to breathe deeply and relax when stressful feelings begin to arise**

   She realized she was becoming upset so she decided to pause, take deep breathes, and address her feeling calmly the next time she becomes angry.

4. **Reword angry feelings so they can be expressed in a non-offensive manner to others**

   Monique will be working on this step. She recognized she lost her cool with Anthony. She apologized and promised to work on her emotions.

5. **Praise yourself for controlling emotional outbursts**

   Hopefully, she felt good because she turned her negative behavior around. Sometimes you have to pat yourself on the back!

☑ checklist

Tips to Handle Anger in a Relationship

 Deal with it as soon as possible

Don't let it build and build. If you do, things will only get worse.

 Get the angry person to talk about why he/she is angry

If you express that you want to help solve the situation, it will get the ball rolling to recovery. Be sympathetic.

Be the calm person

If you can remain calm, it will help the situation. Never fight fire with fire.

Be a good listener

Having someone to vent to gets an angry person on the road to a more relaxed solution.

Don't be afraid to say, "I'm Sorry!"

If you are part of the reason for the angry words, rethink your stance, as well. This one statement can be the fastest solution to ending a stressful situation.

Don't be alone with someone who has yelled or used threatening language towards you

Anger can get out of control very quickly. If the person yells or states (or even hints) that he/she will harm you, avoid being alone together and immediately tell an adult you trust so you can get help to be safe.

The Wired World

We have to be extra careful when communicating in the Wired World. It is always best to talk to someone face-to-face if the topic is of a sensitive or heated nature. You noticed that Monique was able to talk through issues face-to-face with Anthony after she paused, took deep breaths, and calmly stated her points. They had the benefit of seeing and hearing each other. No one else was involved in their discussions.

When you are angry and you post on Facebook or tweet on Twitter, you will probably blurt out whatever comes to mind for the Wired World to see! Later on, you may really regret the words that were released in the atmosphere. So ask yourself, "How would I feel if someone I cared about posted angry and hurtful comments about me?"

If you do not feel right posting something, that's a good sign that you should not! Always try to pause, take some deep breaths, and then calmly talk face-to-face with that person.

Say Whaaat?

"He who angers you, conquers you."
– ELIZABETH KENNY

DANGER SIGNS

Sometimes, one person fears the other person's anger and feels manipulated into doing things just to keep the other person from getting angry. Anger turns really ugly when someone uses it to manipulate and intimidate a dating partner into sexual or other behavior just to "keep the peace." Often, the extreme anger is followed by a "honeymoon period," where the angry person expresses sorrow and promises never to get that angry again. This usually doesn't last – and the anger keeps returning, getting worse over time.

Say Whaaat?

"Be careful of anger – it's just one letter away from danger."

– ANONYMOUS

I Don't Want Us to Break Up

"My boyfriend and I have been dating for a little over a month. He is such a funny, caring and sweet guy. For the past two weeks he has been talking about wanting to have sex. I should add that he is not a virgin, but I am. I'm not ready to take that big step simply because I'm not ready and we've only been together for a month.

I want to sit down with him and have a conversation and tell him how I feel. I just fear that he will try and pressure me into it and I don't want that. Whenever I say 'No, let's wait,' he gets upset, slams things around, and doesn't speak to me for several days. I don't know if I should have sex, and I also don't want him to be angry and break up with me. Help!"

source: thefreedictionary.com

an·ger *noun*
1. A strong feeling of displeasure or hostility.

Whoa! This young woman is squarely in the relationship "danger zone." Her boyfriend is using his anger to manipulate her into doing something that is wrong for her. If he truly cared about and respected her, he'd take her "No" seriously and would stop pressuring her by yelling and giving her the silent treatment.

If she stays in the relationship, she'll just get more of the same. The best thing for her to do now is to confide in an adult she trusts and get advice on how to break up with her boyfriend, before he forces her into sex or causes her physical harm.

CHAPTER 10

TIP ▸ Tenderness

TeNderNeSS
Not TerrorisM (INtiMidation)

My name is Michelle. I live in Paterson, NJ. I'm really upset because I can't hang out with my best friend, Gail, anymore. She has been bringing me down ever since she started dating her "no-good" boyfriend, Brad! Wait! Before you start judging me, you need to know more about my story.

Gail met Brad at our neighborhood skating rink two months ago. He seemed like the perfect boyfriend. He made sure he introduced himself to her parents after the first week of meeting her. He would never call her house after 9 p.m. This guy even opened doors for her. Yeah, a real knight in shining armor – we thought! Well, all of that changed a few weeks ago.

I saw Gail in the parking lot at school one Monday morning getting out of Brad's car. (He has been giving her a ride to school on a regular basis.) I'd said 'hi' and she would glance at me and murmur 'hi' back, and then rush to her first period class. This seemed very strange since Gail and I would usually hang out and gossip about all the stuff we did over the weekend. I thought to myself that she must have been in a hurry to get to class before the bell rang, so I decided to talk to her after school.

As soon as the bell rang for dismissal, Gail raced out of the building and went straight to Brad's car. I could hear him scream, "Hurry up or I will leave your $#$! You know I don't like to wait." She jumped in the car and apologized to him. I tried to call her later that evening, but she made up an excuse for not having time to talk to me.

Okay, so yesterday, I decided I was going to talk to her. I waited for her outside the school doors. Brad pulled into the parking lot and I noticed the two of them arguing about something while seated in his car. He jerked her iPhone out of her hand and wanted to know who she was talking to earlier. I approached the car and told him to stop disrespecting my friend. He cursed me! I told Gail that she deserved better than to be constantly intimidated by a big bully! You know what she said to me? "Mind your own business, Michelle. This is between us!" Can you believe that?

I know what a good relationship should look like. My boyfriend has never raised his voice at me in the seven months we have been dating. In fact, he is very tender and caring towards me. He treats me with respect, values my opinion, and would never try to embarrass or intimidate me. Sadly, after watching Gail and Brad, I am realizing how wonderful it is to be involved in a tender and healthy relationship.

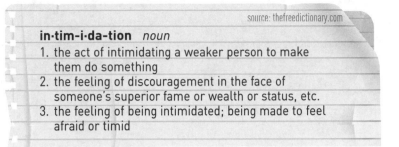

source: thefreedictionary.com

in·tim·i·da·tion *noun*
1. the act of intimidating a weaker person to make them do something
2. the feeling of discouragement in the face of someone's superior fame or wealth or status, etc.
3. the feeling of being intimidated; being made to feel afraid or timid

In healthy relationships, people support each other and are kind and respectful at all times. Gail is involved in a very unhealthy relationship with Brad. Here's why – he controls her by monitoring who she communicates on the phone with. He drives her everywhere so that he can control who she interacts with. He intimidates her by swearing, yelling, and snatching her possessions from her.

In healthy relationships, couples are respectful and readily support each other. They consider the other person's needs and wishes above their own. They are secure in their relationship and do not feel threatened by other people's friendships. In fact, they probably all hang out together from time to time.

Michelle accurately described her relationship with her boyfriend as healthy. He is caring and respectful. She stated that he values her opinion and never tries to intimidate her. These are the characteristics of a person who shows tenderness – not intimidation.

Say Whaaat?

"One of the most sincere forms of respect is actually **listening** to what another has to say."
– BRYANT H. MCGILL

Say Whaaat?

"The first step in getting out of an abusive relationship is to realize that you have the right to be **treated with respect** and not be physically or emotionally harmed by another person."

— DORIS LESSING

RELATIONSHIP SKILL — **SHoWiNg ReSpect**

1. **Stop the negative behavior**

   Brad continued his negative behavior towards Gail. He would snatch her possessions, yell and threaten her. Intimidation is never found in healthy relationships.

2. **Refrain from teasing, threatening, or making fun of others**

   Brad continued his nasty threats and actions. On the other hand, Michelle's boyfriend would never behave in a threatening manner towards her. If he felt that he had offended her, he would immediately apologize to her.

3. **Allow others to have their privacy**

   Gail's phone was snatched from her. Brad invaded her privacy searching through her personal information. If you are involved in a healthy relationship, you must trust your partner and not violate their privacy.

4. Obtain permission before using another person's property

Brad did not respect Gail or any of her wishes. He demonstrated that by snatching personal property away from her.

5. Avoid acting obnoxiously in public

Brad would yell and curse Gail if she did not immediately rush to his car after school. He did not care how rude or obnoxious he was in public. This shows that he had no respect for her and he only wanted to intimidate and control her.

Say Whaaat?

"That you may retain your self-respect, it is better to displease the people by doing what you know is right, than to temporarily please them by doing what you know is wrong.

— WILLIAM J. H. BOETCKER

 The Wired World

It is so important that you are respectful in all you say and do when living in the Wired World. As the relationship skill of respect reminds us, we should refrain from teasing, threats, and making fun of others. When we are communicating through technology, our teasing and jokes can be misconstrued. A simple tease could seem very mean source: thefreedictionary.com

ten·der·ness *noun*
1. a tendency to express warm and affectionate feeling
2. a positive feeling of liking
3. a feeling of concern for the welfare of someone (especially someone defenseless)

or condescending. The skill of respect also asks us to avoid acting obnoxiously in public. This means when we tweet, post, blog, or text message we should check to make sure that the words we send out are thoughtful and not obnoxious or intimidating. Those comments are out there for the entire world to see, and if we really care for the other person we would not want to hurt them.

Sometimes, people use "electronic means" to stalk, harass or intimidate someone. If your significant other asks to see your phone (or takes it from you!) to find out whom you've called or texted, you're being harassed, no matter how much the other person claims to care about you.

DANGER SIGNS

When one person intimidates and threatens another, the relationship is abusive and dangerous – physically and emotionally. Intimidation is a powerful form of manipulation. Unlike jealousy or insecurity, intimidation is not a normal human emotion and has no place in healthy relationships.

The abusive dating partner intimidates by frightening, coercing, or threatening others into submission. Intimidation can be verbal, nonverbal, or a combination of both. Some abusers are quite skilled at intimidating, and getting what they want from others with just a glance or a gesture. Intimidation is always wrong and is always manipulative.

One type of verbal intimidation is threatening. For example, a guy may threaten to hurt his girlfriend or someone close to her, threaten to take one of her favorite possessions and damage or destroy it as a warning of what could happen, or threaten to "tell on" something she has done wrong.

Verbal intimidation is used to make the other person feel uncomfortable and uneasy so the abuser maintains control. Abusers use intimidating and threatening language to "test the waters" to see how much someone will tolerate. These verbal scare tactics often work; the other person becomes too afraid to say "no" and may even worry about his/her safety.

"I'm not mad at you, as long as you're not lying to me. If I find out you are lying, you and me are finished. So, if you're not telling me something, you better spill it now. I don't want to have to find out later from someone else. I can find out!"

"I'm sure I confused the s%#& out of you. One minute I'm mean to you, the next minute I'm whispering I

Say Whaaat?

"Don't smother each other.
No one can grow in the shade."
— LEO BUSCAGLIA

love you while tapping your chest with my water bottle. It was all a play for the girls."

Another form of verbal intimidation is when the abuser uses sexually explicit and/or offensive language when speaking to his/her dating partner. He or she may:

- ◎ Use vulgar sexual language
- ◎ Make sexual noises or sounds (catcalls, howling, barking, etc.)
- ◎ Use specific, graphic sexual descriptions of what he/she wants to do to the other person
- ◎ Ask questions that are too personal or sexual in nature

An abusive dating partner uses graphic or offensive sexual language for various reasons:

- ◎ To scare someone into participating in the described sexual behavior
- ◎ To desensitize his/her target so he or she will become used to this kind of language and eventually this kind of sexual behavior
- ◎ To test a dating partner's limits and boundaries – if the other person laughs, giggles, or even just ignores sexually explicit or obscene language, it gives the abuser the "green light" to continue pushing for sexual activity

Could He Change?

This young woman has fallen for an "emotional terrorist." It's good her family got involved before she was hurt even more.

"Is it possible for someone who is abusive to change? My ex-boyfriend was controlling, jealous, and he has done things that aren't able to be forgiven. I still love him with all my heart and I know I will.

Our families found out what had happened and they won't let us see each other. But I feel like if we were to go to counseling and actually take steps to be better, we could."

 When it comes to relationships, what you see is what you get. Don't ever stay with an abuser hoping he/she will change, because you surely will get hurt in more ways than one.

If someone yells at you, damages property in your presence, or drives carelessly with you in the car, that person is intimidating you and is a threat to your emotional and physical safety. Talk to an adult you trust, and stay far away from that type of abusive behavior.

CHAPTER 11

Encouragement

ENCOURAGEMENT
NOT ENSLAVEMENT (CONTROL)

Christine met Dwayne at "Club Imagination" during spring break. Dwayne spotted her from across the room and could not keep his eyes off her. He immediately walked over to her and started a conversation. They realized they were mutually attracted to each other. Dwayne asked if he could contact her. She answered, yes.

Two weeks later they were going out together – exclusively. Christine very seldom had time to date and had not been in a serious relationship for a while, so her friends were happy she had finally entered the dating scene. Christine even changed her Facebook status from "Single" to "In a Relationship."

As weeks went by, her friends were starting to become concerned because they were seeing less and less of her. They usually studied at Jackson's Coffee House together, but recently she stopped going there because Dwayne wanted her to "hang out" with him. He told her he wants to spend his time with her, not her friends. He even takes her shopping and tells her what clothes and makeup he thinks she should wear.

DATING!

Christine recently found out she was chosen to participate in a regional debate competition in Philadelphia. She was thrilled, so she shared the news with Dwayne. He immediately told her he thought she should not go to a "stupid event" like that. He said he hated debates and he would not come to see it. Christine was hurt and became angry. She was starting to see Dwayne did not want a girlfriend; he wanted a puppet he could manipulate and control.

At first she thought he was so sweet to want to be with her all the time. She now feels pressured, enslaved, and unable to be herself. She realized her friends had always encouraged her, while Dwayne was extremely discouraging and belittling. Christine decided it was time to become assertive by having a "talk" with Dwayne about his controlling behaviors. She calmly, yet firmly, told him she wanted her independence and friends back. He tried to make her feel guilty for speaking her mind and expressing her feelings. She took a few deep breaths, and calmly stood her ground.

"I have become increasingly closed off from my friends and the things I love. I have been feeling like a puppet, but today I am cutting the strings to this relationship," she told him.

In healthy relationships, people encourage each other's independence and realize they don't "own" each other. Dwayne expressed his control over Christine through possessive and belittling words and behaviors. He didn't want anyone else "messing" with his "territory." He attempted to control who she talked to, how she dressed, and even how she spent money. He acted as if he completely owned her feelings and behaviors and was resentful and extremely

Say Whaaat?

"Some of the biggest challenges in relationships come from the fact that many people enter into a relationship in order to get something: they're trying to find someone who's going to make them feel good. In reality, the only way a relationship will last is if you see **your relationship** as a place that **you go to give,** and not a place that you go to take."

— ANTHONY ROBBINS

jealous of anyone who got any kind of attention from his "possession."

Treating someone like an object to own, rather than a person to relate to, is at the heart of jealousy and possessiveness. You may see and hear signs of this everywhere: "She's my woman," "You can't talk to him," "You belong to me," and so on. But remember, people are not objects to be owned or possessed or controlled.

Keep in mind there's a fine line between someone enjoying your company and wanting to spend time with you, and a dating partner who monopolizes your every moment and monitors your every move. While you want to have "quality time" with your boyfriend/girlfriend (free from distractions like texting, phone calls, tweeting, or Facebook), you also need to give each other freedom to "do your own thing," too.

In healthy relationships, partners support and encourage each other's independence. They are not threatened by others and do not treat their partner like a possession. Christine finally realized that Dwayne was controlling her

– not encouraging her. She would rather have a "Single" status and be happy, rather than be "In a Relationship," and feel trapped.

source: thefreedictionary.com

con·trol *noun*
1. Authority or ability to manage or direct
2. a. One that controls; a controlling agent, device, or organization.
   b. An instrument or set of instruments used to operate, regulate, or guide a machine or vehicle. Often used in the plural.
3. A restraining device, measure, or limit; a curb

RELATIONSHIP SKILL — ASSertiveNeSS

1. **Look at the person**

   When Christine finally decided to have a "talk" with Dwayne, she talked to him – face to face.

2. **Use a neutral, calm voice**

   She kept her voice at a low calm level.

3. **Remain relaxed and breathe deeply**

   Christine took a few deep breaths before speaking to Dwayne.

4. **Clearly state your opinion or disagreement. Avoid emotional terms**

   She calmly and firmly stated that she wanted her independence back.

   She stood her ground. Good for her!

ENCOURAGEMENT

5. Listen to the other person

Although she was not in agreement with what Dwayne had to say, she listened to his side of the story.

The Wired World

Sometimes, relationships can get a little crazy in the Wired World. People are too eager to change their relationship status on Facebook from "Single" to "In a Relationship." Please take your time and see how things go before making those declarations. Because once you put them out there, people will be watching to see how long it lasts. Final note: do not let any one person manipulate or hoard all of your time via text, Skype, Instagram, or any other method. If your boyfriend or girlfriend insists you "check in" all the time (or at specific times) or if he or she "monitors" who you call, text, or "talk to" online, you're being controlled and manipulated. Your best bet is to do what Christine did – assert yourself and your rights. Talk to an adult you trust, and end the relationship.

DANGER SIGNS

How do you know if you're being limited or manipulated by your dating partner? Check out this list:

Someone is too controlling if he or she:

- Calls constantly to check up on you
- Tells you how to dress, who to hang out with, how to spend your time or money
- Forces or manipulates you into doing what he or she wants

- Sends harassing or threatening e-mails, messages, or notes
- Physically, emotionally, or sexually abuses you
- Uses violence or intimidation to get his or her way
- Humiliates or puts you down in public
- Makes demands or gives orders
- Tries to get you to keep the relationship a secret
- Has an explosive temper – throws objects, slams doors, punches walls, etc.
- Refuses to listen to or show respect to you and others
- Attempts to keep you away from friends or family
- Gives gifts to get something from you in return
- Spreads rumors about you
- Threatens suicide or self-harm

Say Whaaat?

"Correction does much, but encouragement does more."
– JOHANN WOLFGANG VON GOETHE

en·cour·age·ment *noun*
1. The act of encouraging.
2. The state of being encouraged.
3. One that encourages.

Hello, I would call but I don't want to wake up my parents. I don't know what to do anymore. I've been with this guy for three months. It's a controlling relationship. I feel like I can't even talk to my guy friends. He has my Facebook password. I feel like I don't even have a life. He gets mad that I vent to my friends about him because I am unhappy. He guilt trips me and makes me feel like complete crap.

He makes me feel selfish and that everything is my fault and never his. He tells me things like I am being manipulating when I am not what so ever. I don't even know how to be manipulating. It makes me cry and feel crappy. I know this relationship is BAD, but I just can't get out of it. I don't know what to do. He does not like for me to be with my friends. He thinks that he owns me! I can't deal with this anymore. I've been so depressed. I have thought about harming myself a few times, but I haven't done it because I am stronger.

I just don't know how much longer I can deal with him before I actually end up doing something to myself because of the way he makes me feel.

Whoa! This young woman feels desperate. She's right to fear her boyfriend – he's controlling her like a possession he owns instead of a person with rights and feelings. She's on track to getting her life back now that she recognizes how bad things have gotten. The best thing for her to do is to wake up her parents and come clean – they can help her get away from him and stay safe.

CHAPTER 12

TIPS

Kind Intentions * Compliments * Gifts
Similarities * Generosity * Self-Assurance
Accuracy * Serenity * Tenderness
Encouragement

Summary
Relationship Status

Remember Marcus and Shania from Chapter one? They got it right. After dating for nearly a year, they can look back and see how far they've come and how glad they are they didn't rush things. They let the relationship grow while giving each other plenty of space.

Being thoughtful, taking it slow and learning respect for each other wasn't easy, but because they cared so much for each other, it's gotten easier over time. Several other couples in this book have applied some basic principles to their relationships, but Marcus and Shania have committed to all of them. Here are the ten principles or tips that Marcus and Shania have practiced with each other; now we'll share them with you:

1. Kind Intentions – In Chapter 2, Cody and Katie discovered that kindness was an essential ingredient in maintaining their relationship. Cody liked Katie's smile and kindness towards him. Katie loved his

blue eyes and honest ways. Likewise, Marcus
and Shania expressed their kindness through
encouragement and saying nice things about
each other.

2. Compliments – In Chapter 3, David complimented
Tamika's wit, knowledge, and personality. He
was also impressed with her concern for others.
After realizing that David was sincere with his
compliments, Tamika began to develop positive
feelings towards him. They became "exclusive
friends" afterwards. Remember, Shania
complimented Marcus on his wonderful singing
voice. He frequently complimented her on how
pretty she looked. Sincere compliments played an
important role in their newfound relationship.

3. Gifts – In some relationships, people think that they
need to impress their friend with expensive gifts. In
Chapter 4, Karon believed that Greg would be more
attracted to her if she gave him an expensive watch.
She did not realize that all Greg wanted was the
gift of time and attention. Her smile and friendship
would have served as a great gift to him. She ended
up "turning off" Greg because she used gifts as a
way to bribe him. Marcus and Shania gladly use
phone calls, compliments, and time together as their
sentimental gifts to each other.

4. Similarities – Shania and Marcus discovered they had
so many things in common. They loved basketball
games, choir, working for the school newspaper,
and hanging out with friends. Because they had
so many similar interests, there was little room for
disagreements. Keep in mind; it's healthy to have
some different hobbies and interests. Having some
differences create opportunities for couples to share
and learn from each other. Problems often arise

when couples have nothing in common (i.e. age, interests, or friends).

5. Generosity – Couples must learn to be generous with their time, attention, friends, and family. Mala (in Chapter 6) learned what Marcus and Shania had already figured out – a lack of generosity and sharing can lead to jealousy and possessiveness. Shania explained to Marcus he would have to come over and meet her family before she would go out with him. He spent time getting to know Shania's father. He now has a strong relationship with her dad. They also spent time together with friends.

6. Self-Assurance – Couples who care about each other are each other's "biggest fans." They offer encouragement and their dating partners, like Maria and Arturo in Chapter 7, feel an increased sense of self-confidence.

7. Accuracy – If you care about someone, you don't let your thoughts run away with you. If you have a suspicion or concern, you share your concern calmly, like Lynette did with Eric in Chapter 8, and then listen to the other person's side of the story before rushing to unfair or damaging accusations.

8. Serenity – Everybody feels anger at some time or another. It's normal and human! In healthy relationships, though, people don't use their anger to control their partners. Like Monique, in Chapter 9, caring dating partners learn to control and think through their feelings before they say or do something hurtful that they'll regret later.

9. Tenderness – In Chapter 10, Gail's boyfriend, Brad, is emotionally abusive. He stalks her, yells at her, and is keeping her away from her friend Michelle. Michelle knows this isn't right – in good

relationships, dating partners treat each other with kindness and respect (and treat their family members and friends that way, too).

10. Encouragement – Last, but not least, couples who care about each other never try to intimidate or control each other. They encourage each other's outside interests and friendships, and don't use fear or threats, like Christine's boyfriend Dwayne did in Chapter 11, to force the other person to "obey."

So – can you change your status from "Single" to "In a Relationship" without getting hurt or losing yourself? The good news here is you can – if you just remember you need to work at **being** the right person before you set out to **find** the right person. The first step is setting your own boundaries.

Healthy relationships start with healthy boundaries. When you know how to choose good dating partners, you can enjoy dating, discover new things about yourself, and avoid lots of "drama." First, though, you need to learn how to set healthy boundaries for yourself and to respect others' boundaries as well.

WHat are BouNdaries?

There's a certain healthy physical and emotional distance that you keep between yourself and others. This distance is often referred to as your "boundaries." Boundaries define where you end and where someone else begins. They help you to recognize what is, and what is not, your responsibility in relationships.

Imagine a series of invisible circles around your physical and emotional self. These circles determine how close you will let people get to you. These circles represent the

TYPES OF BOUNDARIES

1 External

External boundaries protect your body, keeping it safe and healthy. External boundaries have two components – physical and sexual. Physical boundaries protect your body, and sexual boundaries protect your sexual body parts and your sexuality.

2 Internal

Internal boundaries protect your thoughts and emotions. Internal boundaries have two components – emotional and spiritual. Emotional boundaries help you protect your feelings, and spiritual boundaries help you protect the deepest part of who you are – your sense of hope, trust, mystery, security, and sense of spirituality.

various kinds of boundaries we all have. Boundaries help you determine how much you will share with others and how open or emotionally and physically close you will be with all the various people in your life.

Boundaries work in two ways – they let people in, and they keep people out. Boundaries protect your thoughts, feelings, body, and behavior. They help tell you what's right and wrong.

Say Whaaat?

"Love can sometimes be magic.
But magic can sometimes... just be an illusion."
– JAVAN

Learning about Boundaries

You begin learning about and setting boundaries at an early age. Your parents help teach you right from wrong, as well as how and who to be physically and emotionally close with. When you were young, your parents probably had all kinds of rules for you, like "Look both ways before crossing the street" or "Don't talk to strangers." Both of these rules are also boundaries, designed to help you protect your physical, emotional, sexual, and spiritual self.

As you grow older and begin to develop more and more relationships outside your family, you begin to put what you've learned about boundaries into practice. Think about emotional boundaries for a moment. In your family, you probably learned to trust your parents and brothers and sisters enough to tell them your personal thoughts and feelings. As we grow older, most people continue to share their private thoughts and feelings only with family and best friends.

People with healthy boundaries are selective about whom they allow inside their closest emotional and physical boundaries. They know that most relationships, like those with casual acquaintances or classmates, are not as personal and therefore it would not be wise to share personal thoughts, feelings, or experiences within such relationships. Not enough trust has been established. Casual acquaintances should talk about "light" and non-personal topics like the weather, sports, movies, schoolwork, or current events.

People with healthy boundaries would also never consider telling strangers about personal information. They learned long ago that "Don't talk to strangers" was a good boundary designed to protect them. As a teen or young adult, you may occasionally talk to strangers, but only about the time, sports, weather or directions – never about anything personal.

As an example of physical boundaries, think about riding in an elevator alone. You have all that space to yourself, and you can move around as you please. Gradually, other people get on the elevator. You're not as comfortable as when you were alone. More people get on the elevator; someone steps on your foot, you feel scrunched in a corner. You feel uneasy because other people have entered the space where you once felt comfortable. They are just too close. They have crossed your physical boundaries.

Physical boundaries, or comfort zones, change depending on the relationship and may also change over time as the relationship changes. Think about going on a first date. This person is a casual acquaintance. If your boundaries are healthy, you probably would not feel comfortable getting too close. But after several dates, you may trust the other person enough to hold hands, slow dance, or even hug.

Boundary Crossing

In the elevator example, the people were strangers. Had they been your friends, you may not have felt as uncomfortable. But the same uncomfortable feeling of having your boundaries "crossed" can occur in friendships and other close relationships, too. Friends and even family members can violate your boundaries. When friends or family violate your trust, they also violate your boundaries.

Some boundary violations include:

- Interrupting a conversation
- Taking one of your possessions without permission
- Teasing or making fun of you
- Asking very personal questions
- Gossiping about others
- Touching your body without your permission
- Telling other people stories about you
- Telling other people private information about you
- Always being around you – making you feel uncomfortable by invading your "private space"
- Using offensive, vulgar, or sexually explicit language in your presence
- Forcing you into doing something sexual
- Physically abusing you

Say Whaaat?

"Love looks through a telescope; envy, through a microscope."
– JOSH BILLINGS

So what should you do when someone crosses or violates your boundaries? Think of a soccer or basketball game. What happens when the ball goes out of bounds? The game stops for a few seconds. The team and the coaches may even meet to decide what to do next.

It's a lot like that in life, too. When someone crosses one of your boundaries, whether it is a stranger, friend, or family member, you need to step back from the situation and decide what to do next. It may help to talk to someone else you trust about what happened. Describe the situation, as well as how you feel. Ask for help deciding what to do next. In most cases, it's important to tell the person who violated your boundary what he or she did and how it was hurtful to you.

Usually, an apology from the boundary crosser can go a long way toward rebuilding trust and the relationship. But remember, some boundary violations are serious enough that you should never let that person emotionally, physically, sexually, or spiritually close to you again.

Boundary Problems

Appropriate boundaries protect a person's physical, sexual, emotional, and spiritual self. But when appropriate boundaries aren't set, it can create a dangerous situation where you could get hurt or end up hurting someone else.

Your boundaries are too open if you:

* Can't say "no"
* Share too much personal information
* Take responsibility for others' feelings
* Allow yourself to be abused

✳ Reveal personal thoughts, feelings, or experiences to acquaintances or strangers

✳ Believe you deserve bad treatment

✳ Can't see flaws in others

✳ Will do anything to avoid conflict

✳ Engage in public displays of affection

✳ Wear revealing or seductive clothing (including sagging pants)

✳ Stand or sit too close to others

✳ Make sexual comments, jokes, or noises in public

✳ Trust strangers

✳ Believe everything you hear

✳ Have sexual encounters with acquaintances or strangers

Your boundaries are too closed if you:

★ Always say "no" to requests that might require you to get close to somebody

★ Share little or nothing about you

★ Are unable to identify your own wants, needs, and feelings

★ Don't have any friends

★ Don't let adults help

★ Never ask for help, even when needed

★ Refuse to let trustworthy adults touch you appropriately (handshakes, pats on the back)

Boundary Questionnaire

How do you know if a relationship has unhealthy boundaries? A careful reading and discussion of the topics in this book should give you a pretty good idea of what an unhealthy relationship looks like and sounds like. The following questions can help you take a closer look at your friendships and dating relationships. Be honest with yourself as you answer these questions. These questions may help point out unhealthy qualities in some of your relationships.

Think about your closest friends (or your boyfriend or girlfriend):

- Does this person try to tell me what to do, how to dress, who to hang out with?

- Do I spend most of my time worrying about this relationship?

- Does it seem that this person purposefully tries to make me feel jealous or insecure?

- Does it seem that I do all the giving and my friend does all the taking?

- Does my friend put unrealistic demands on me? What demands?

- Does my friend ignore me or attempt to control me when others are around? What usually happens?

- Does it seem like this friend is always trying to change me? How?

- Does my friend purposefully do things to hurt me emotionally or physically? What?

- Do other people tell me that my friend talks behind my back? About what?

- Do I get into trouble when I do what my friend says? How?

- Do I feel ashamed, guilty, or afraid after talking or being with this person?

- Have I quit doing things that I used to enjoy since I've become involved with this person? What? Why?

- Does this person ever threaten or intimidate me?

- Has this person ever given me a gift and expected sexual contact in return?

A "yes" to any of these questions points to an unhealthy characteristic in your friendship. The more "yes" answers you gave, the more unhealthy qualities your friendship has. Take some time to figure out if you can correct what's going wrong (or if the friendship is worth it). On the other hand, a lot of "no" answers indicate that you and your friend have a good friendship. See what you can do to make it even better.

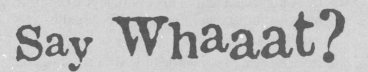

Say Whaaat?

"The little unremembered acts of kindness and love are the best parts of a person's life."
— WILLIAM WORDSWORTH

 **checklist**

What to Do

If you feel you've been used or abused in a relationship, there are a number of steps you can take:

 ### Tell someone who can help

Talk to someone you trust – a parent, a professional counselor, teacher, or other adult who will listen and offer help.

Understand that change is possible

You're not weird or crazy. What happened was not your fault; someone took advantage of you. It's time to begin a new life that's free from abuse.

Be honest

Admit that something bad happened to you. Don't make excuses for yourself or the person who used you. Don't hide the secret anymore. The pain will never stop if you don't do something about it. Let the pain end so the healing can begin. You could call the Boys Town Hotline® at 800-448-3000.

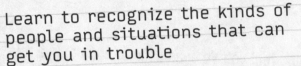

Learn to recognize the kinds of people and situations that can get you in trouble

Do some problem solving to find ways to avoid or get away from abusive people and negative environments.

Learn how to create and maintain healthy boundaries

Read all you can about healthy boundaries and friendship. Observe people who have good boundaries and healthy friendships. Take notice of what makes good relationships grow. Then put into practice what you've learned.

Learn healthy responses to stress

Things may worry you; people may upset you. Get involved in positive activities. Exercise. Doing kind and helpful things for others will help you avoid getting bogged down in self-pity.

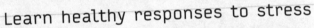

Setting appropriate Boundaries

There are many ways to set and maintain appropriate boundaries. The following tips can help you set good boundaries:

▽ Identify peers and adults you can trust and build relationships with them

▽ Avoid people who are selfish, disrespectful, manipulative or abusive

▽ Spend time with people who do well in school and at home, who are liked and respected by many people

▽ Learn to say "no" when you're being pressured to do something wrong

▽ Trust your sense of safety or danger

▽ Learn how to think through and solve problems before reacting

▽ Think about times when your personal boundaries were violated

▽ Speak up when someone or something bothers you

▽ Set limits about where you will go, what you will do, and how long you will be there

▽ Find ways to tell (or show) others what your personal boundaries are

DATING!

Rules For Good Boundaries

Different kinds of relationships have different kinds of boundaries. Your physical, emotional, sexual, and spiritual boundaries with your parents and siblings are different than the boundaries you have with friends. The boundaries you set with a stranger should be different than the boundaries you have with classmates or co-workers.

Below are some good points to consider as a relationship or friendship is developing. These are general rules you can follow that can help you establish and maintain good boundaries in all your relationships.

Length of time – How long have you known this person? How can knowing someone longer be beneficial to you? How long is long enough before a stranger becomes a friend? How do you decide?

Knowledge about the other person – What, and how much, do you really know about this person? Some important things to know about someone you are considering dating are:

- How does this person react when given "no" for an answer?
- How does this person handle frustrations and disappointments?
- How does he or she express anger?
- How does this person treat his or her parents?
- How does this person speak about and treat the other gender?

Sharing activities – How many different kinds of activities have you shared together? What are they? How have these experiences helped you get to know the other person better?

Amount of self-disclosure – How much personal information have you shared? How much has the other person shared? Are you comfortable with the sharing? Why or why not? Is the amount of sharing equal between the two of you?

Number of different experiences – What has this person experienced in life? How has it affected him or her? What can this person's experiences tell you about him or her?

Role appropriate – We all have certain roles in life. Some roles are not compatible for dating or friendship relationships. Teachers shouldn't date students; doctors should not date patients, etc. What role does this person have in your life?

Age appropriate – As a teen, friendships or dating relationships with those more than two years older or younger than you can be harmful. What is the age difference between you? If it is greater than two years, how could this be harmful?

Level of reciprocal trust – Can you trust this person? How do you know? Are you worthy of his or her trust? Why? How do you know when someone is trustworthy? What happens when trust is broken?

EXpLaiNiNg tHe rULeS

Length of Time

When developing a new relationship, remember that time is on your side! Really getting to know someone takes time. It doesn't happen overnight. Never rush into a relationship or allow someone to rush you. Take it gradually. If it is good and healthy boundaries are respected, it will last.

DATING!

Knowledge about the Other Person

Getting to know someone involves spending "real" time together, (not just "virtual time" chatting on the computer) as well as talking about many things – his or her family, likes and dislikes, hopes and dreams for the future, past experiences, etc. If you are considering a close relationship with someone, there are some really important things you should know about including: How does this person react when hearing "no" for an answer? How does he or she treat brothers, sisters, and parents? How does he or she speak about the opposite gender when with friends? How does this person handle frustrations and anger?

You can learn such important information not only by discussing these issues but also by observing how he or she interacts with others. This is why group dating can be helpful. It allows you to see the other person interact with a variety of people.

Amount of Self-Disclosure and Trust

How much personal information should you share with someone you are just getting to know? The best rule of thumb is to share a small bit of personal information, something you wouldn't really mind if others found out about. Then see what happens. If he or she respects you and your boundaries, then your personal information won't become public news. But if he or she does share your personal information with others, it's a sure sign that this person is not trustworthy.

How do you know if someone is really trustworthy? Remember that real trust is built. It takes time. It is something we prove through our actions, not just something we say with words. A trustworthy person is someone who keeps his or her promises, who is there for you in good times and in bad, and who tells you the truth even when it's hard.

Trust is hard earned but easily broken. Sometimes even our family and closest friends will break our trust and violate our boundaries. When that happens, an apology with appropriate amends can go a long way toward rebuilding trust and repairing the relationship.

Role and Age Appropriate

We all have certain roles in life. Some roles are incompatible for dating relationships or even friendship. Teachers should not date or seek students out as friends. Doctors should not date patients. Coaches should not date or seek out the athletes they coach as friends. Certain relationships are designed to be dependent, where one person has more knowledge, power, or status than the other. Because of their dependent nature, these types of relationships are considered role inappropriate and not conducive to dating or friendship relationships.

Does age really matter? When you're a teenager, yes. During adolescence, dating someone more than two years older or younger can be at the very least problematic or in the worst-case scenario, illegal, harmful, and dangerous. Consider the differences between the life experiences of someone in seventh grade and someone in twelfth grade. Think about how you have changed physically and emotionally in the last few years.

Looking for Balance

Remember that a healthy friendship or a dating relationship should always involve give and take from both people. That doesn't mean you should keep a scorecard of what you and your friends do for one another, but it is a good idea to see if there is a healthy balance. Evaluate the relationships you have now and try to find that balance.

It's also good to keep in mind that friendship and dating are just one portion of life. Spending too much time thinking about one relationship takes away from all of the other important things you should be concentrating on. Make sure you take care of the responsibilities you have to your family, school, church, and community. Your friends should respect your choice to do so.

Realize that friendships and dating relationships will change; some will change for the better, some for the worse. Learn how to adjust to these changes without giving up the things you believe in. Strive to be flexible and understanding of others while sticking with the things you know are right.

Look at past relationships that were positive. Make a list of the things that made those relationships healthy. Identify any positive changes friends have helped you make in your life. Then name the things you do to help make positive changes in others. Always make sure you are encouraging one another to change for the better.

It may also help to examine relationships that didn't work out. Although relationships are a two-way street, try to figure out what part you played to make each relationship end up the way it did. Remember what you learned from past relationships so that you can avoid those mistakes in the future.

Relationships are not random. Who we befriend and date are not accidents of fate. When it comes to relating, and especially dating, there are choices and decisions to be made long before we ever meet that special person. Knowing yourself, understanding what makes for a good or a bad relationship, being sure of your values and boundaries, and practicing good social skills will set the stage for healthy friendships and dating relationships now and in the future.

All this thought and preparation may seem less than romantic. But try thinking about it this way – it is within healthy relationship boundaries that a real and lasting romance can flourish.

About the Authors

Laura J. Buddenberg, MS, PLMHP
Manager, Training and Community Outreach

Laura Buddenberg joined the Boys Town staff in 2000. In her capacity as Manager, Training and Community Outreach, she works with staff, children, and families on issues relating to parenting, relationships, bullying, and the role of faith in family life. She is co-author of five books, and appears regularly on radio and television to share Boys Town parenting tips and strategies. Laura holds a Master of Science degree in Family and Youth Services, as well as a provisional mental health practice license and a Certificate in Family Life Ministry. She and her husband Roger have been married for 29 years and are the parents of two young adult daughters.

Alesia King Montgomery
National Senior Training Consultant

Alesia King Montgomery has worked for Boys Town for 25 years in a variety of roles. In her current role as National Senior Training Consultant, she trains and consults to teachers and administrators throughout the country. In her community, she conducts empowerment workshops for teens and adults, has mentored young teenagers through her role as an advisor within the Zeta Phi Beta Sorority, and counseled families in her local church. She graduated from Tuskegee University, and was born in Birmingham, AL. She and her husband Greg are the proud parents of an adult daughter, Jessica.